New D

GW00992129

Edited by Sally Welch   September–December 2016

New Daylight © BRF 2016

The Bible Reading Fellowship
15 The Chambers, Vineyard, Abingdon OX14 3FE
Tel: 01865 319700; Fax: 01865 319701
E-mail: enquiries@brf.org.uk; Website: www.brf.org.uk

ISBN 978 0 85746 396 8

Distributed in Australia by Mediacom Education Inc., PO Box 610, Unley, SA 5061.
Tel: 1800 811 311; Fax: 08 8297 8719;
E-mail: admin@mediacom.org.au
Available also from all good Christian bookshops in Australia.
For individual and group subscriptions in Australia:
Mrs Rosemary Morrall, PO Box W35, Wanniassa, ACT 2903.

Distributed in New Zealand by Scripture Union Wholesale, PO Box 760, Wellington
Tel: 04 385 0421; Fax: 04 384 3990; E-mail: suwholesale@clear.net.nz

Publications distributed to more than 60 countries

Acknowledgments
The New Revised Standard Version of the Bible, Anglicised Edition, copyright © 1989, 1995 by
the Division of Christian Education of the National Council of the Churches of Christ in the
USA. Used by permission. All rights reserved.

The Holy Bible, New International Version, Anglicised edition, copyright © 1979, 1984, 2011
by Biblica. Used by permission of Hodder & Stoughton Publishers, an Hachette UK
company. All rights reserved. 'NIV' is a registered trademark of Biblica. UK trademark
number 1448790.

The Holy Bible, New Living Translation, copyright © 1996, 2004, 2007, 2013. Used by
permission of Tyndale House Publishers, Inc., Carol Stream, Illinois 60188. All rights
reserved.

Scripture taken from THE MESSAGE. Copyright © 1993, 1994, 1995, 1996, 2000, 2001, 2002.
Used by permission of NavPress Publishing Group.

Extracts from *The Book of Common Prayer of 1662*, the rights of which are vested in the
Crown in perpetuity within the United Kingdom, are reproduced by permission of
Cambridge University Press, Her Majesty's Printers.

The Revised Common Lectionary is copyright © The Consultation on Common Texts, 1992
and is reproduced with permission. *The Christian Year: Calendar, Lectionary and Collects*,
which includes the *Common Worship* lectionary (the Church of England's adaptations of the
Revised Common Lectionary, published as the Principal Service lectionary) is copyright © The
Central Board of Finance of the Church of England, 1995, 1997, and material from it is
reproduced with permission.

Printed by Gutenberg Press, Tarxien, Malta.

Suggestions for using *New Daylight*

Find a regular time and place, if possible, where you can read and pray undisturbed. Before you begin, take time to be still and perhaps use the BRF prayer. Then read the Bible passage slowly (try reading it aloud if you find it over-familiar), followed by the comment. You can also use *New Daylight* for group study and discussion, if you prefer.

The prayer or point for reflection can be a starting point for your own meditation and prayer. Many people like to keep a journal to record their thoughts about a Bible passage and items for prayer. In *New Daylight* we also note the Sundays and some special festivals from the Church calendar, to keep in step with the Christian year.

New Daylight and the Bible

New Daylight contributors use a range of Bible versions, and you will find a list of the versions used opposite, on page 2. You are welcome to use your own preferred version alongside the passage printed in the notes. This can be particularly helpful if the Bible text has been abridged.

New Daylight affirms that the whole of the Bible is God's revelation to us, and we should read, reflect on and learn from every part of both Old and New Testaments. Usually the printed comment presents a straightforward 'thought for the day', but sometimes it may also raise questions rather than simply providing answers, as we wrestle with some of the more difficult passages of Scripture.

New Daylight is also available in a deluxe edition (larger format). Visit your local Christian bookshop or contact the BRF office, who can also give details about a cassette version for the visually impaired. For a Braille edition, contact St John's Guild, Sovereign House, 12–14 Warwick Street, Coventry CV5 6ET.

Comment on *New Daylight*

To send feedback, you may email or write to BRF at the addresses shown opposite. If you would like your comment to be included on our website, please email connect@brf.org.uk. You can also Tweet to @brfonline (please use the hashtag #brfconnect).

Writers in this issue

Amy Boucher Pye is an American who has lived in the UK for over a decade. She makes her home in North London with her husband and young family and enjoys writing for Christian magazines.

Michael Mitton is Fresh Expressions Adviser for Derby Diocese, NSM Priest-in-charge of St Paul's Derby and honorary Canon of Derby Cathedral. He is the author of *Travellers of the Heart* (BRF, 2013).

Nick Read is an Anglican priest, Agricultural Chaplain with Borderlands Rural Chaplaincy and Director of the Bulmer Foundation (www.bulmerfoundation.org.uk). Married to Julie, a parish priest in Herefordshire, he lives in one of the most rural parts of Britain.

David Winter is retired from parish ministry. An honorary Canon of Christ Church, Oxford, he is well known as a writer and broadcaster. His most recent book for BRF is *Heaven's Morning.*.

Barbara Mosse is a retired Anglican priest with experience in various chaplaincies. A freelance lecturer and retreat giver, she is the author of *Welcoming the Way of the Cross* (BRF, 2013).

Rosemary Lain-Priestley has been a priest in the Church of England for 18 years. She is an advocate for the ministries of female clergy. She is also the author of three books and the mother of three children.

Veronica Zundel is an Oxford graduate, writer and journalist. She lives with her husband and son in North London, where they belong to the Mennonite Church.

David Runcorn is a writer, spiritual director, theological teacher, retreat leader and conference speaker. He lives in Gloucester. You can meet him at www.davidruncorn.com.

Amanda Bloor is a Director of Ordinands in the Diocese of Oxford. She enjoys reading feminist theology and undertook research into how people develop priestly identities. In her spare time she is a chaplain to Oxfordshire Army Cadet Force.

Ian Adams is a poet, writer, photographer and priest working with themes of spirituality, culture and community. He is the creator of Morning Bell (Twitter @pacebene), and author of *Running Over Rocks* (Canterbury Press, 2013).

Sally Welch writes...

One of the peculiarities of editing *New Daylight* is that I read a fort-night's reflections at one sitting. The authors send in their work more or less at the specified deadline, whereupon I read through each set of contributions, making minor editorial corrections, making sure that each piece is the right length, checking the Bible version, and so on. This is a bit of a pity, in a way, as it means I am not able to give each day's reflection the proper amount of time to study it or use it as a basis for prayer or personal reflection. On the other hand, I get a wonderful picture of the whole series, as the individual reflections build one on the other, leading me to new insights and understand-ing. If you are able, I recommend that, at the end of each series, you take the time to read them through as a whole; I guarantee you will encounter new meanings and material to ponder. This is especially the case with Ian Adams' Christmas reflections: I have already con-gratulated him on the way he has found new insights in a story that is so dear, yet so familiar. With that familiarity comes the danger that we might overlook its significance for our world.

We begin this issue with Amy Boucher Pye's sensitive exploration of the letters of Paul to Timothy. We can be too distracted by Paul's atti-tude to women in these letters really to understand and appreciate the rest of their content, which Amy demonstrates as being full of sensible and loving advice to new and developing churches. We would do well to look to this advice in today's congregations and communities. This issue also contains a contribution from a new writer, Nick Read, who has spent many years ministering in deeply rural parts of Herefordshire. His series on farming in the Bible is wise and heartfelt in its plea for deeper understanding of the issues facing agriculture today.

I have aimed for a broad range of topics and approaches, using writ-ers with different styles and methods of sharing their knowledge and insight. I have been in turn challenged, taught, delighted and encour-aged; my prayer is that you too might find the same richness within this issue of *New Daylight*.

Sally Welch

The BRF Prayer

Almighty God,
you have taught us that your word is a lamp for our feet
and a light for our path. Help us, and all who prayerfully
read your word, to deepen our fellowship with you
and with each other through your love.
And in so doing may we come to know you more fully,
love you more truly, and follow more faithfully
in the steps of your son Jesus Christ, who lives and reigns
with you and the Holy Spirit, one God for evermore.
Amen

Paul's letters to Timothy

The apostle Paul sometimes gets a bad rap, with people saying that he is misogynistic, harsh and didactic. Perhaps he is seen this way because they forget that we are only reading half of the conversation. If we do not consider the bigger picture, we might be confused as to why Paul would tell the people from one church that they needed to tighten up (the Corinthians), yet tell the people from another that they should loosen up (the Galatians). When we delve more deeply into the clues in the letters and those in the book of Acts, however, we can grow to understand Paul's heart and hopes not only for the gospel but also that those in the early church would grow and flourish.

In his letters to Timothy, Paul writes to a younger man whom he has mentored. In his first letter, he knows that Timothy faces the effect of false teachers who are leading people astray. Such is the level of his concern that he uses strong language to encourage Timothy to root out the heresy and lead the people into the ways of truth and life. He instructs him about church life and how the leaders should live, as well as how they should treat the widows in their midst.

This first letter to Timothy also contains a controversial passage in which Paul forbids women to speak in church (2:11–15). I have not included it in the notes here. This is partly because our space is limited—in contrast to the doctoral dissertations, articles and books in which people have written at length on the subject—but also I do not want to impose my view on you in your daily engagement with the Bible.

As we will see, Paul wrote his second letter to Timothy after writing to Titus, when he was still concerned about the influence of false teachers. By the time of this final letter, that crisis seems to have passed, but now Paul faces execution in Rome at the hands of Nero. His letter to the man he mentored, whom he now sees as an equal, contains his last words. He sums up the charge he leaves to Timothy as he embraces his final homecoming.

I pray our journey into these pastoral letters will enrich, challenge and encourage you.

AMY BOUCHER PYE

Our goal

As I urged you when I went into Macedonia, stay there in Ephesus so that you may command certain people not to teach false doctrines any longer or to devote themselves to myths and endless genealogies. Such things promote controversial speculations rather than advancing God's work—which is by faith. The goal of this command is love, which comes from a pure heart and a good conscience and a sincere faith. Some have departed from these and have turned to meaningless talk. They want to be teachers of the law, but they do not know what they are talking about or what they so confidently affirm.

False doctrines, myths and endless genealogies—the apostle Paul instructs Timothy once again to stay where he is so that he can speak against the teachers who, he says, do not know what they are talking about. Paul does not mince his words on this point, but does not then concern himself with rules either. Instead, what he is keen to stress is the importance of love, which, he says, is the goal of the life of faith.

I wonder what Paul would say to Christians today. Have we, on the one hand, become too worked up over naming false teaching or, on the other, embraced myths and, thus, meaningless talk? Do we land somewhere in between? No doubt we all veer one way or another at times, so we need a dose not only of humility but also the indwelling of the Holy Spirit to keep us walking in step with God.

We can ask the Lord to make love our goal, helping us keep a pure heart, a good conscience and a sincere faith. As he moulds us, he may gently reveal the stances we grasp too strongly or the areas in our lives that we need to tighten up. His correction is soaked in love, not condemnation, making it all the easier to welcome and receive.

Purify my heart, Lord, and cleanse my conscience, that my works might bring you glory and spread your love. Amen

AMY BOUCHER PYE

The power of story

Even though I was once a blasphemer and a persecutor and a violent man, I was shown mercy because I acted in ignorance and unbelief. The grace of our Lord was poured out on me abundantly, along with the faith and love that are in Christ Jesus. Here is a trustworthy saying that deserves full acceptance: Christ Jesus came into the world to save sinners—of whom I am the worst. But for that very reason I was shown mercy so that in me, the worst of sinners, Christ Jesus might display his immense patience as an example for those who would believe in him and receive eternal life. Now to the King eternal, immortal, invisible, the only God, be honour and glory for ever and ever. Amen.

The apostle Paul could have written the original 'triumph over tragedy' story—the killer who was blinded by the light, transformed and changed, then sent to love the ones he had persecuted. Though his life was not always smooth sailing, he never forgot who he had been and who—and whose—he now was. As he says to Timothy, he was once a violent slayer of God's followers, but even he was redeemed and renewed, becoming one to whom God promised eternal life because of his great mercy and love.

Paul's reference to his being the sinner made new shows the power of narrative and testimony, for, as his life shows, the Lord can effect lasting change. He is no longer a blasphemer or persecutor, but one filled with faith and love, and he cannot contain his worship for the God who saved him (v. 17).

Whether our history includes stories of betrayal and heartbreak or those of love and acceptance, we can join Paul in his song of praise for the one who deserves our honour and reverence.

'But thanks be to God that, though you used to be slaves to sin, you have come to obey from your heart the pattern of teaching that has now claimed your allegiance. You have been set free from sin and have become slaves to righteousness' (Romans 6:17–18).

AMY BOUCHER PYE

Prayer and authority

I urge, then, first of all, that petitions, prayers, intercession and thanksgiving be made for all people—for kings and all those in authority, that we may live peaceful and quiet lives in all godliness and holiness. This is good, and pleases God our Saviour, who wants all people to be saved and to come to a knowledge of the truth. For there is one God and one mediator between God and mankind, the man Christ Jesus, who gave himself as a ransom for all people.

Last year, Queen Elizabeth II surpassed Queen Victoria as the longest-reigning monarch of the United Kingdom. As an American who is now also her subject, I have harboured mixed feelings and views about the monarchy over the years, but I am humbled by the Queen, who has served her country tirelessly as part of her duty and calling. It is an honour to pray for her and her reign.

We might feel jolted by Paul's command to Timothy to pray for rulers and kings, coming so early on in this letter of instructions for Timothy. Paul, however, yearns for the gospel to be proclaimed and accepted and he knows that a just and ordered society, rather than one with a culture of corruption, will foster its message as one that people can hear and heed. Note, too, the various ways in which Paul wants the people to pray—through 'petitions, prayers, intercession and thanksgiving' (v. 1)—for he knows that God hears our prayers.

How can we pray for our rulers today and this week, that our societies may enable people to thrive in freedom and faith? Perhaps you could join with others from your neighbourhood or church, once a month or once a term, to pray for your local and national leaders. We trust that God hears us and responds.

Lord God, you are the ultimate ruler, just and fair. We give you thanks for those in authority over us, praying that they will embody the values of wisdom, justice and mercy. Amen

AMY BOUCHER PYE

Christ is all

Although I hope to come to you soon, I am writing to you with these instructions so that, if I am delayed, you will know how people ought to conduct themselves in God's household, which is the church of the living God, the pillar and foundation of the truth. Beyond all question, the mystery from which true godliness springs is great: he appeared in the flesh, was vindicated by the Spirit, was seen by angels, was preached among the nations, was believed on in the world, was taken up in glory.

As Paul moves from his opening remarks to addressing the false teaching that has abounded in the church at Ephesus, he does not want to lose sight of Jesus. Theologians differ in their views on the form and structure of the hymn of praise in verse 16, but the content is clear—the second person of the Trinity shapes our faith and practice. We may not fully understand the mystery of God becoming man and returning to heaven, but we know that through his dwelling in us we can bear the fruit of goodness and godliness.

Take a moment to consider the words of the ancient song, such as 'He appeared in the flesh'. As the opening of John's Gospel puts it, 'The Word became flesh and made his dwelling among us. We have seen his glory, the glory of the one and only Son, who came from the Father, full of grace and truth' (John 1:14). Our God, through Jesus, is fully acquainted with the feelings we experience, such as joy and grief.

The rest of the hymn also reflects his dual nature of God and man. For instance, as a man he has been preached among the nations and believed by millions around the world. In terms of his being God, angels have seen him and he was taken from earth into heaven.

How does Jesus' dual nature—divine and human—affect you?

'The true light that gives light to everyone was coming into the world...
Yet to all who did receive him, to those who believed in his name, he
gave the right to become children of God' (John 1:9, 12).

AMY BOUCHER PYE

Training in godliness

If you point these things out to the brothers and sisters, you will be a good minister of Christ Jesus, nourished on the truths of the faith and of the good teaching that you have followed. Have nothing to do with godless myths and old wives' tales; rather, train yourself to be godly. For physical training is of some value, but godliness has value for all things, holding promise for both the present life and the life to come. This is a trustworthy saying that deserves full acceptance. That is why we labour and strive, because we have put our hope in the living God, who is the Saviour of all people, and especially of those who believe.

The trend of the yearned-for perfectly shaped and sculpted body continues in our culture as we run, train, jump, pump iron, dance and eat foods according to the latest diet, whether low or high GI, protein or something else. Do we focus enough, though, on the training of our soul? Do we have fit bodies but fat minds, as the memorable title of Os Guinness' book has it (*Fit Bodies, Fat Minds*, Baker, 1994)?

Paul speaks of Timothy being nourished by the food that lasts—that is, the truths of the faith and the good teaching he has received, whether through his mother and grandmother, church leaders or Paul himself. Why, Paul says, should we neglect the state of our souls in favour of the state of our bodies, when it is our souls that will live on into eternity?

Many Christians seek to practise spiritual disciplines regularly, such as Bible reading and study, being thankful, taking time for silence and solitude and doing good deeds in secret. They often find doing so in community to be mutually beneficial, too. May we continue to spur each other on towards love and good deeds (Hebrews 10:24).

Father God, through the power of your Holy Spirit, help us to train ourselves in righteousness, that we might reflect your grace and your glory to a hurting world. Amen

AMY BOUCHER PYE

The work of elders

The elders who direct the affairs of the church well are worthy of double honour, especially those whose work is preaching and teaching. For Scripture says, 'Do not muzzle an ox while it is treading out the grain,' and 'The worker deserves his wages.' Do not entertain an accusation against an elder unless it is brought by two or three witnesses. But those elders who are sinning you are to reprove before everyone, so that the others may take warning. I charge you, in the sight of God and Christ Jesus and the elect angels, to keep these instructions without partiality, and to do nothing out of favouritism.

The Church of England may have its faults, but, as one with vested interests in it (I'm married to an Anglican vicar), I think its system of paying the clergy works well in principle (notwithstanding those families in which the spouse does not work, who may struggle financially). For all clergy are paid roughly the same stipend, whether theirs is a large church or a tiny one, and the wealthier churches pay into a central fund that finances churches in poorer areas. With a standard stipend, the clergy are not tempted to move from post to post to seek a larger salary.

Paul touches on this issue of not playing favourites in his letter to Timothy, although he emphasises Timothy's actions regarding the elders—namely how he should act wisely, impartially and with justice. They are to be remunerated for their work, Paul says, but they are also to be held to account. I wonder if Paul was picturing the elders as he wrote his letter, for he had spent three years at the church in Ephesus previously.

It is beneficial to consider the work of the elders, not least so that we can pray for and support those in positions of church leadership. Clergy friends say how much they value the prayers of the people in their congregations, even—perhaps especially—when there are points on which they are divided.

What do you think is behind Paul's command to 'not entertain an accusation against an elder unless it is brought by two or three witnesses' (v. 19)?

AMY BOUCHER PYE

Enough

But godliness with contentment is great gain. For we brought nothing into the world, and we can take nothing out of it. But if we have food and clothing, we will be content with that. Those who want to get rich fall into temptation and a trap and into many foolish and harmful desires that plunge people into ruin and destruction. For the love of money is a root of all kinds of evil. Some people, eager for money, have wandered from the faith and pierced themselves with many griefs.

Some ask, 'How much is enough?' Another will answer, 'Just the next deal/conquest/thing to buy.' The human heart wants and yearns for fulfilment and when we are not seeking God to fill those empty spaces, we all look to all sorts of other things to fill the void, such as money to buy us stuff—for social status, ease or convenience or other forms of gratification.

Note that, in the text, Paul says that the love of money can lead to evil—not that all money leads to evil, nor that money itself is evil. Rather, he is speaking about the state of people's hearts, what it is they are desiring. As they plot and plan about acquiring the next thing, they can find it increasingly difficult to resist temptation, which can lead to ruin. Paul, in contrast, counsels being content with what we have. After all, we cannot take any of our stuff with us into the next life. The Lord would have us seek instead his love, peace and joy as the source of true riches to share.

I have met people who do not have many material possessions and have a stingy attitude. Equally, I have met people with a lot of money who are not only generous but also do not seem to be defined by their worldly wealth. As Paul says, it is all down to the state of our hearts.

Over to you. How much is enough?

Father God, we yearn for contentment; we yearn for you. By your Holy Spirit, fill the places in our souls that feel empty and void, that we might desire aright. Amen

AMY BOUCHER PYE

Habits of the heart

But you, man of God, flee from all this, and pursue righteousness, godliness, faith, love, endurance and gentleness. Fight the good fight of the faith. Take hold of the eternal life to which you were called when you made your good confession in the presence of many witnesses. In the sight of God, who gives life to everything, and of Christ Jesus, who while testifying before Pontius Pilate made the good confession, I charge you to keep this command without spot or blame until the appearing of our Lord Jesus Christ, which God will bring about in his own time—God, the blessed and only Ruler, the King of kings and Lord of lords, who alone is immortal and who lives in unapproachable light, whom no one has seen or can see. To him be honour and might for ever. Amen.

As Paul brings his letter to its conclusion, he warns Timothy not to act as the false teachers do, but to 'fight the good fight of the faith' (v. 12). Note his list of spiritual practices that he wants Timothy to embrace: to flee ungodliness, pursue righteousness, take hold of eternal life, and keep the commands Paul has given him. We are to live out the gift of life in the kingdom of God every day, employing our wills, minds and bodies.

Paul, in his other letters, often speaks of putting off the old self and putting on the new (see Ephesians 4:22–24, for example), again emphasising this practice as an active one. Living in the fallen world as we do and being subject to our sinful nature, we need to put on the new self daily. We may do so through such actions as confession and receiving forgiveness, asking for God's help in making wise and godly choices and filling our minds with his words.

For we know, as Paul says, that our God is the only ruler, king and Lord. He is immortal and unapproachable, but makes the way clear for us to rest in his love.

Father God, I pray that you will help me shed any of my habits that are unhealthy, so I might live out of my redeemed self. Amen

AMY BOUCHER PYE

Last testament

I thank God, whom I serve, as my ancestors did, with a clear conscience, as night and day I constantly remember you in my prayers. Recalling your tears, I long to see you, so that I may be filled with joy. I am reminded of your sincere faith... For this reason I remind you to fan into flame the gift of God, which is in you through the laying on of my hands. For the Spirit God gave us does not make us timid, but gives us power, love and self-discipline. So do not be ashamed of the testimony about our Lord or of me his prisoner. Rather, join with me in suffering for the gospel, by the power of God. He has saved us and called us to a holy life.

Paul opens his second letter to Timothy in a gentler manner than his first. Many biblical commentators think that, by the time he wrote this letter, the crisis with the false teachers had passed, which Paul addressed not only in 1 Timothy but also in Titus. He probably wrote this letter four years after he wrote 1 Timothy, dictating his words while in chains during his second spell of imprisonment in Rome, not long before his execution. These are therefore his last words to his beloved friend—one whom he mentored in the faith; one for whom he prays 'night and day' (v. 3) and longs to see one last time.

In 1 Timothy, Paul emphasises our part in working out our faith in practice. In this letter, he also highlights the role of God's transforming power. For instance, Timothy should 'fan into flame' (v. 6) the gifts that God has given him. Although Timothy may take the initial action, a power other than he brings about the result. Just as wind will stoke a fire, the Lord will blow his Spirit into Timothy to yield the gifts of power, love and self-discipline as Timothy pursues a holy life.

May the triune God fan into flame our faith.

'Is not my word like fire,' declares the Lord, 'and like a hammer that breaks a rock in pieces?' (Jeremiah 23:29).

AMY BOUCHER PYE

Faithful in the task

You then, my son, be strong in the grace that is in Christ Jesus. And the things you have heard me say in the presence of many witnesses entrust to reliable people who will also be qualified to teach others. Join with me in suffering, like a good soldier of Christ Jesus. No one serving as a soldier gets entangled in civilian affairs, but rather tries to please his commanding officer. Similarly, anyone who competes as an athlete does not receive the victor's crown except by competing according to the rules. The hardworking farmer should be the first to receive a share of the crops. Reflect on what I am saying, for the Lord will give you insight into all this.

Paul fills his letters with vivid images that stick in the mind and imagination. As he passes along to Timothy his final words of wisdom and his longings for the fulfilment of the gospel, he uses examples from ancient times that Timothy would have been familiar with—a soldier, athlete and farmer. Those working tirelessly for the gospel may not appear to reap the same concrete results as those growing crops or winning races, but Paul trusts that Timothy will understand his examples as the Lord gives him insight.

The three examples have in common that hard work and faithfulness are needed to produce a result: soldiers follow in obedience; athletes submit their bodies to training; farmers cultivate and care for the land. Each of the three show their commitment in their training, devotion and consistency. So too, infers Paul, should Christians commit to their lives of godliness and right living.

Note that soldiers, athletes and farmers do not know in advance what the end results of their efforts will be—whether a battle or competition will be won or lost, or a harvest will be good or bad. Their faithfulness and dedication to the task is what matters.

Lord God, we may be at the beginning of our journey in life with you, at the end or somewhere in the middle. Wherever we are on this road, we ask you to help us to be faithful, for your glory. Amen

AMY BOUCHER PYE

Godless chatter

Keep reminding God's people of these things. Warn them before God against quarrelling about words; it is of no value, and only ruins those who listen. Do your best to present yourself to God as one approved, a worker who does not need to be ashamed and who correctly handles the word of truth. Avoid godless chatter, because those who indulge in it will become more and more ungodly. Their teaching will spread like gangrene. Among them are Hymenaeus and Philetus, who have departed from the truth. They say that the resurrection has already taken place, and they destroy the faith of some. Nevertheless, God's solid foundation stands firm.

Seemingly without taking a breath, Paul's tone changes and he returns to the brisk warnings against false teaching that he made in 1 Timothy and Titus. He may be making his final remarks in this letter, but he reserves the right to warn Timothy against the results of the distractions of idle talk and endless controversies, saying it will 'spread like gangrene' (v. 17)—a memorable image. Although God's truth is the solid foundation, never to be worn down by rust or mould—or eaten away by gangrene—those in church leadership can become infected, their focus diverted from the teaching, preaching and serving that should occupy them. Paul yearns that Timothy, and those who follow after him, would be saved from those trials.

I have heard stories about and witnessed church conflict, including 'godless chatter' and quarrels over words. Soon the arguments descend into character assassinations, with opponents leaving the language of love far behind. How the Holy Spirit must grieve over such divisions.

Consider taking a few moments to review in your mind and heart, and before God, any conflicts at church you have been involved in. May we echo King David, who said, 'How good and pleasant it is when God's people live together in unity' (Psalm 133:1).

Lord Jesus, you died so that we might find you and friendship with our neighbours. May your grace oil the wheels of communication in our homes, our churches and wherever we meet others.

AMY BOUCHER PYE

Holy writ

But as for you, continue in what you have learned and have become convinced of, because you know those from whom you learned it, and how from infancy you have known the Holy Scriptures, which are able to make you wise for salvation through faith in Christ Jesus. All Scripture is God-breathed and is useful for teaching, rebuking, correcting and training in righteousness, so that the servant of God may be thoroughly equipped for every good work.

Many Christians memorise 2 Timothy 3:16 and I can understand why, for it is the strongest statement about the Bible made in the Bible. Reading this statement on its own, however, out of the context of Paul's letters to Timothy, dilutes its impact. As we have spent nearly a fortnight considering these missives, we can put them in that context and gain a sense of the power of Paul's view of the Bible. This crescendo at the end of the two letters reveals how he knows its worth in church life, especially when dealing with false teaching.

We can take comfort and courage, knowing that scripture is 'God-breathed' (v. 16) and, as Hebrews 4:12 says, 'alive and active. Sharper than any double-edged sword, it penetrates even to dividing soul and spirit, joints and marrow…' With the Holy Spirit's inspiration, when we read the Bible we can hear God speaking to us—in words of love and affirmation, conviction and direction. As Paul says, we will find teaching there and, sometimes, the sense of being rebuked and corrected. Through it all we will be given the tools to do the works of God.

Dallas Willard, a renowned writer on the spiritual disciples, prized the practice of memorising scripture and would regularly commit long passages to memory. He even said if one had to choose between a 'quiet time' and memorising, he would choose the latter. When we do so, we find God's word more readily available in our hearts and minds.

May we become wise for salvation through faith in Jesus Christ.

Lord Jesus Christ, you are the Word made flesh. May you bring us wisdom as we read the scriptures, that we may serve you and reach out to those in need. Amen

AMY BOUCHER PYE

Preach the word

In the presence of God and of Christ Jesus, who will judge the living and the dead, and in view of his appearing and his kingdom, I give you this charge: preach the word; be prepared in season and out of season; correct, rebuke and encourage—with great patience and careful instruction. For the time will come when people will not put up with sound doctrine. Instead, to suit their own desires, they will gather round them a great number of teachers to say what their itching ears want to hear. They will turn their ears away from the truth and turn aside to myths. But you, keep your head in all situations, endure hardship, do the work of an evangelist, discharge all the duties of your ministry.

As we come to the end of Paul's letter, he lays out his final commands to Timothy, underlining their importance as he calls on the Father and Son as his witnesses. His exhortations reflect his understanding that Timothy in his ministry will again encounter false teaching—he is to preach, be prepared, correct, rebuke, encourage. As we saw earlier, Timothy should do this with love—with great patience.

'Keep your head,' Paul says (v. 5). A simple charge, but one we all should heed, for when we lose our cool, we can descend into words we should not speak and actions we should avoid. Anger can turn into bitterness and rage as we lose our self-control, which can quickly negate our good work of sharing the gospel. I think with shame of the times when I have lost my cool.

Instead, taking Paul's advice, we can be prepared 'in season and out' (v. 2), training ourselves with the help of the Holy Spirit to exercise self-control in times of ease and abundance, so that later, in moments or seasons of stress and hardship, our character reflects Christ.

My prayer is that we would be given great patience and great love.

Lord God, may our teachers bring you glory with sound teaching, winsome words and a deep reservoir of patience. May we also love to learn. Amen

AMY BOUCHER PYE

Finishing the race

For I am already being poured out like a drink offering, and the time for my departure is near. I have fought the good fight, I have finished the race, I have kept the faith. Now there is in store for me the crown of righteousness, which the Lord, the righteous Judge, will award to me on that day—and not only to me, but also to all who have longed for his appearing.

When one of my mentors died, I saw it as a mercy. Never filled with glowing good health, and longing for heaven, she felt she had come to the end of her earthly life. She had completed her mission—having passed over her Christian organisation to other gifted people—and was ready to die. I imagine she could have echoed Paul's words as the time for her departure grew near, that she, too, had been 'poured out like a drink offering' (v. 6).

When he was writing this letter, Paul must have known that he would not escape imprisonment and would soon be executed. He again employs the language of an athlete as he says that he has finished the race, fought the good fight and soon will receive the crown of righteousness. He seems content even though his earthly life is drawing to a close.

As we conclude our fortnight with Paul, with him writing right before his death, consider how in our culture we often do all that we can to avoid thinking about dying—including employing such phrases for the dead as 'passed away' or 'gone to be with Jesus'. We may feel ambivalent about dying or would be sad not to fulfil our dreams if we were to die soon, but we can ask the Lord for peace and reassurance. Like Paul, may we one day be able to say that we have run the good race and finished our mission.

'The Spirit and the bride say, "Come!" And let the one who hears say, "Come!" Let the one who is thirsty come; and let the one who wishes take the free gift of the water of life' (Revelation 22:17).

AMY BOUCHER PYE

Ecclesiastes

Ecclesiastes is arguably the strangest book in the Bible. At first sight it seems to be the rambling thoughts of an ageing cynic who has been around the block too many times. We delight in the beautiful pieces of writing, we laugh at the pithy proverbs, but we can find ourselves discomfited by the pessimistic view of life that all is vanity and we are chasing after the wind. A protest rises up in us that, in God, life is full of meaning. Perhaps this is exactly what this curious writer is aiming to do—provoke us into questioning and exploring so that we discover for ourselves the real meaning of life.

The writer calls himself Qoheleth, which is difficult to translate. Traditionally he is called Ecclesiastes (the word refers to 'gathering', in terms of gathering wise sayings), but others have gone for Preacher, Philosopher and Teacher. Eugene Peterson, in *The Message*, calls him the Quester, reflecting the writer's rugged determination to be utterly authentic and honest about the questions life throws at us. Whatever name we give him, though, he will not tolerate off-the-peg official answers to the big questions of suffering and injustice. He is prepared to live in the questions, rather than rush to quick answers as a way of avoiding awkward issues. His aim is to help us join him in thinking honestly about our experience of life.

We can feel frustrated by the fact that he asks more questions than he offers answers, but that is because the book is an invitation to us to think for ourselves. The book also serves to expose the silly and super-ficial ways of living that are a temptation to all of us. It tells us that, on our own, we make a poor attempt at trying to make sense of this life.

Eugene Peterson, in his introduction to Ecclesiastes, says that the book serves as a bath, not a meal: 'We read Ecclesiastes to get scrubbed clean from illusion and sentiment.' A few buckets of Ecclesiastes rinse away any notion that we can have life on our terms. In the end, it is about trusting God, with a trust that is rooted in honest searching, not wishful thinking.

MICHAEL MITTON

Vanity of vanities

Vanity of vanities, says the Teacher, vanity of vanities! All is vanity. What do people gain from all the toil at which they toil under the sun? A generation goes, and a generation comes, but the earth remains for ever. The sun rises and the sun goes down, and hurries to the place where it rises. The wind blows to the south, and goes round to the north; round and round goes the wind, and on its circuits the wind returns.

Qoheleth pulls no punches. Right from the start, he states his conviction loud and clear: all is vanity. In fact, not just vanity, but 'vanity of vanities' (v. 2). Just as 'holy of holies' is a term to express utter holiness, so 'vanity of vanities' expresses utter meaninglessness and emptiness. He is drawing alongside all those who have had experiences that have caused them to question the very meaning of life. He is not the preacher who stands in the pulpit telling the people they must move from their despair to hope. He has come down to their level and is showing profound empathy with them. He sits down with all who are asking serious questions about life, the universe and God. Those who suffer debilitating doubts and questioning find in Qoheleth a companion who is a brilliant reflective listener, giving words to thoughts they hardly dare utter. It is comforting to find such questions right at the heart of our scriptures.

Qoheleth then asks a question that sounds very like the question Jesus asks in Mark 8:36: 'What will it profit them to gain the whole world and forfeit their life?' Jesus asks this just after teaching about taking up the cross. Qoheleth, by coming alongside us in our questions, is urging us to think about what is really valuable in this world. We need no reminders that today we live in a world that is terribly confused about what is truly valuable. This ancient teacher's voice is remarkably contemporary. He will guide us to that which is truly valuable, as opposed to merely chasing after the wind.

Lord, let me be honest about my questions, that I may discover your wisdom. Amen

MICHAEL MITTON

Living the life of Riley

I made great works; I built houses and planted vineyards for myself; I made myself gardens and parks, and planted in them all kinds of fruit trees. I made myself pools from which to water the forest of growing trees. I bought male and female slaves, and had slaves who were born in my house; I also had great possessions of herds and flocks, more than any who had been before me in Jerusalem.

In chapter 2 of his book, Qoheleth tells us of his quest to find meaning through many different pleasures of this world, the fruits of his hard work. Reading his words today, we could be reading one of those magazines that delight in telling us of the lives of celebrities with their fast cars, big houses, beautiful partners and fabulous wealth. Those of us for whom such wealth can only be dreamed of may look on them with apparent disapproval, yet we may also secretly imagine that such wealth would bring security and peace of mind. Yes, we all know that celebrities can be as unhappy as any of us, but the attraction of the material world is strong nevertheless.

Qoheleth taps into this human instinct for wealth and security, but then exposes it as chasing after the wind (v. 11). 'You long for this?' he effectively asks us. 'Well, so have I, and it does not work.' If there is a bit of us that still says, 'I wouldn't mind testing it', it shows there is work still to be done in our hearts!

Lest we think Qoheleth will then commend a life of abstinence, he doesn't. In verses 24–26, he tells us that many of the pleasures of life come from the hand of God. What spoils these pleasures is trying to get out of them more than they can give. In verse 26, Qoheleth gives us a hint as to what will lead us to wisdom: pleasing God. He has discovered that there is something inbuilt in the human spirit that finds its deepest peace in serving the Creator.

Why should pleasing God bring greater peace and security than prosperity and material security?

MICHAEL MITTON

Where does the time go?

He has made everything suitable for its time; moreover, he has put a sense of past and future into their minds, yet they cannot find out what God has done from the beginning to the end. I know that there is nothing better for them than to be happy and enjoy themselves as long as they live; moreover, it is God's gift that all should eat and drink and take pleasure in all their toil. I know that whatever God does endures for ever; nothing can be added to it, nor anything taken from it; God has done this, so that all should stand in awe before him.

The opening verses of chapter 3 are some of the most beautiful and profound words on time ever written. As he reflects on life, Qoheleth discerns a rhythm—of life, death, weeping, laughing, mourning, dancing. Nothing settles for too long. We find ourselves carried from one kind of experience to its direct opposite and often such movements are quite outside our control. There is nothing we can do about the advance of time, for example. We throw up our hands again and again, saying, 'How time flies!' We can easily start to live as though we are at the mercy of time and its changes, but Qoheleth reminds us that God is behind all of this. It is he who has put an understanding of time into our minds. For that reason, we are not at the mercy of time, but, in God, we have control.

Qoheleth helps us to see that all this change does not need to be unsettling or cause despair—it is a sign of God's energy in the world. Everywhere there are signs of his divine patterns. We are not meant to live in high summer all the time; if we will but trust God, even the winters and dark times have their beauty and gifts to offer. Qoheleth is taking us to one of the strong themes of his book: the way of peace is about trusting God, the author of all seasons.

---

*Why is it that we are so often surprised by the speed
at which time passes?*

MICHAEL MITTON

The weight of oppression

Moreover, I saw under the sun that in the place of justice, wickedness was there, and in the place of righteousness, wickedness was there as well. I said in my heart, God will judge the righteous and the wicked, for he has appointed a time for every matter, and for every work. I said in my heart with regard to human beings that God is testing them to show that they are but animals. For the fate of humans and the fate of animals is the same.

In his teaching on time, Qoheleth assures us that God is in control of all seasons of life. But sooner or later someone will point out that there are people on this earth who suffer terrible injustice, and their winter season seems endless. The second part of chapter 3 and the beginning of chapter 4 lament the fact that we live in a world of extreme injustice. It is a subject that concerns Qoheleth deeply and he returns to it several times in his book. As he explores the dreadful human capacity to inflict hurt, he comes close to despair: such humans behave like animals (3:18) and the truly blessed ones are those who have never been born, so they have not seen such things (4:3).

It is comforting to find someone in scripture who knows what it is to feel so downcast by injustice and cruelty. We are not alone. We read news reports of atrocities—some perpetrated in the apparent safety of home, others in the war-ravaged cities of foreign lands. Our hearts sink and our faith falters at such reports. Qoheleth is there with us; he takes hold of our hands and says, 'But God will judge all, and he has appointed a time for it.' So, although we grieve in the harsh days of waiting, there is comfort in knowing that one day, one glorious day, all the cruelties of this earth will be judged by the only one who knows how to judge justly.

Oh my Lord, I see such suffering in this world caused by my fellow humans. Lead me to prayer, to action and to trust in your judgements.
Amen

MICHAEL MITTON

The rat race

Then I saw that all toil and all skill in work come from one person's envy of another. This also is vanity and a chasing after wind. Fools fold their hands and consume their own flesh. Better is a handful with quiet than two handfuls with toil, and a chasing after wind. Again, I saw vanity under the sun: the case of solitary individuals, without sons or brothers; yet there is no end to all their toil, and their eyes are never satisfied with riches.

Qoheleth now turns his gaze to some very restless people—those who are driven by envy or obsessed with wealth. Though written several thousand years ago, it is clear that this early society struggled with much the same problems we do, and nothing much changes under the sun!

Any who say that the Bible is an out-of-date book need to read Qoheleth's words and learn from his observations of human nature. He notices that, in some people, their drivenness comes from their envy of others and a competitive nature, always wanting to be ahead of others. If he were alive today, he would not be surprised by the overtaking manoeuvres of some road users. He would wander into our shopping centres and watch the seductive ways of our consumer society and nod his head knowingly. Such human instincts run deep and have done so for centuries.

Qoheleth simply wants us to stop and ask serious questions about how we behave, especially about getting sucked into ways of living that, in the end, are as empty as the wind. If he saw our frantic busy-ness, he would come along and say, 'Better is a handful with quiet than two with toil' (v. 6) and suddenly the spell that drives us to be overly busy would be broken. We are invited to step back, be still and come back to our senses. Today is a new day and an opportunity to pause and open our hands to receive that quiet, so that we can be restored to being all God made us to be.

When you are overly busy, what is it that is driving you? How can you make space to open your hands to the quietness of God?

MICHAEL MITTON

The wisdom to listen

Guard your steps when you go to the house of God; to draw near to listen is better than the sacrifice offered by fools; for they do not know how to keep from doing evil. Never be rash with your mouth, nor let your heart be quick to utter a word before God, for God is in heaven, and you upon earth; therefore let your words be few.

The middle chapters of Ecclesiastes are a collection of reflections and home truths that develop Qoheleth's early questions and explorations. Tomorrow we shall start looking at his conclusions, but today we pause with some words he writes about coming to the place of worship. His advice is beautifully simple: when you come to worship, come primarily to listen.

In the Old Testament Wisdom literature, the 'fools' are those who fail to learn wisdom. They have opted to live at a shallow level, focused on themselves and indifferent to the ways of God. Any of us can be foolish or wise—the choice is ours.

In the case of worship, the fools are those who come to God in a busy state of mind, wanting to sing their hymns and songs, hear a good sermon and generally feel better. The wise are those who come with a sense of expectation, knowing that a word from the Lord could change their lives. Qoheleth teaches that to learn such attentiveness in the house of God produces an awareness of God in heaven, sharing wisdom with us on earth. As a result, our words become fewer but wiser.

We will all have varying experiences of church, but one of the best things that can happen in church is for us to find a stillness of heart that opens us to the word of God. Qoheleth teaches us that such listening produces a wisdom that will then spill out to others in our daily lives. Going to church with this expectation can open us to whole new adventures.

'The wise old owl sat on an oak; the more he saw, the less he spoke. The less he spoke, the more he heard. Why aren't we like that wise old bird?'

Oliver Wendell Holmes
MICHAEL MITTON

The wisdom of being adventurous

Send out your bread upon the waters, for after many days you will get it back. Divide your means seven ways, or even eight, for you do not know what disaster may happen on earth. When clouds are full, they empty rain on the earth; whether a tree falls to the south or to the north, in the place where the tree falls, there it will lie. Whoever observes the wind will not sow; and whoever regards the clouds will not reap.

In previous chapters, as we have seen, Qoheleth discusses the many ways in which humanity chases after the wind. The news seems to be more bad than good, but, once we move into chapter 11, the prevailing mood becomes one of hope.

Qoheleth has been utterly realistic about the many paradoxes of human life and behaviour, but he has constantly been directing us to put our roots in the fear of God (such as in 8:12). In doing so we are washed of the seductions of this world and start to gain a better perspective. From here, we can start to be truly daring.

Qoheleth invites us to cast our 'bread upon the waters'—a risky thing, as no one knows what might happen to it. Yet, it will be productive, he says. Our knowledge of how fragile our days are on this earth should make us generous. If we are rooted in the wisdom of God, we will not be spending our time anxiously looking at the wind, but getting out there and sowing new seed. Qoheleth tells us that the kind of wisdom he is commending will lead us to become bold adventurers in this life.

There is something very radical in his approach. He invites us to look at the worst things about life, but, in the end, encourages us to live it to the full. His way is to be realistic about the darkness of this world and our own lives, yet to draw our attention to our unchangeable and dependable, if very mysterious, God. Wisdom is realistic about the tough questions of life, but is able to exist with them even if they are not answered.

Lord, open my heart to wisdom, that I may adventure with you. Amen

MICHAEL MITTON

The wisdom to enjoy life

Light is sweet, and it is pleasant for the eyes to see the sun. Even those who live for many years should rejoice in them all; yet let them remember that the days of darkness will be many. All that comes is vanity. Rejoice, young man, while you are young, and let your heart cheer you in the days of your youth. Follow the inclination of your heart and the desire of your eyes, but know that for all these things God will bring you into judgement. Banish anxiety from your mind, and put away pain from your body; for youth and the dawn of life are vanity.

There is a passage similar to this in Ecclesiastes 9:7–12, where, to use *The Message*'s paraphrase, Qoheleth encourages us to 'Seize life! Eat bread with gusto… God takes pleasure in *your* pleasure!' He may have explored the dark side of life, but he has no intention of ignoring the bright side.

Our passage today is full of paradoxes. Qoheleth encourages us to rejoice in the years we have, but at the same time remember that the days of dark death will be many. The young man should enjoy his youth, but also remember that God will bring him into judgement. There is no need for young people to be anxious, but then youth and early life are all vanity. It almost sounds as if we can be happy, but with provisos.

What Qoheleth is doing is telling us that true enjoyment of life comes with a proper perspective. If a young man simply eats, drinks and is merry without a sense of 'judgement', he will fritter away his youth and it will all be a chasing after the wind. If, however, he is a proper steward of a wonderful stage of life, knowing that it only lasts a short time, then there is genuine joy to be had. Qoheleth's God is not a spoilsport judge, curbing our attempts to be happy, but one who wants to lead us to genuine and lasting contentedness.

Think about moments in your life when you have known genuine joy.
How can you 'seize life' today?

MICHAEL MITTON

The breath of life

Remember your creator in the days of your youth, before the days of trouble come, and the years draw near when you will say, 'I have no pleasure in them'; before the sun and the light and the moon and the stars are darkened and the clouds return with the rain... before the silver cord is snapped, and the golden bowl is broken, and the pitcher is broken at the fountain, and the wheel broken at the cistern, and the dust returns to the earth as it was, and the breath returns to God who gave it.

We come to the final words of Qoheleth, and he ends his book with the advice of an old man to a young one. Seldom have we found more beautiful words on the sense of decline experienced in old age. This speech might have come from a Shakespearean tragedy where an aged hero steps to the edge of the stage and opens the door of his heart for one last time before he rests in peace.

For the aged Qoheleth, his last words to the youth are a warning: life hurries by at quite a pace, so make the most of each day that is given. Before the losses of old age happen, enjoy life to the full. Qoheleth is well aware that death is not far away for him: the silver cord will be snapped, his precious 'golden bowl' will be broken and the dust will return to the earth. Of course, this is a reference to the dust of Genesis 2:7 and 3:19. We were formed from the dust and we return to the dust, and thus we are reminded of the creation and fall story.

Today's passage may seem a sad reflection on the decline of old age, but what shines out radiantly from this book is that, in spirit, Qoheleth is far from declining; he is flourishing. How else could he write such brilliant words of wisdom? The Creator is with him every day of his life, right to the very day when his breath will return to God (Ecclesiastes 11:7).

Creator God, fill me with the breath of life today and all my days.
Amen

MICHAEL MITTON

Getting the message

The sayings of the wise are like goads, and like nails firmly fixed are the collected sayings that are given by one shepherd. Of anything beyond these, my child, beware. Of making many books there is no end, and much study is a weariness of the flesh. The end of the matter; all has been heard. Fear God, and keep his commandments; for that is the whole duty of everyone. For God will bring every deed into judgement, including every secret thing, whether good or evil.

The final verses are written by an editor who commends Qoheleth to us, encouraging us to see that such words of wisdom work as both goads and nails. That is, they provoke us and probe our shallow thinking, but can also provide security and hold the fabric of our lives together. We are also told that such wisdom comes from the shepherd. To use such an image of God helps us to know that these words, though they may seem sharp at times, are from a pastoral God, whose intention is for us to grow and flourish.

The editor then quickly brings the book to an end, warning that you can study too much. He does not go, however, before he gives one final summary of Qoheleth's message: 'Fear God, and keep his commandments' (v. 13). Translators usually include the word 'duty' in verse 13, but it is not actually in the Hebrew. The sense is that to fear God makes us whole: it brings us all to our full, whole humanity. To fear God is to recognise that he oversees this great mystery of life and knows every part of us and our world, the good and ill of everyone. He understands light and darkness.

So, to use Peterson's analogy (see notes for 14 September), by reading through Ecclesiastes, we have had a good bath. Quick and simplistic answers to the vexing problems of life have been washed away; our silly attempts to find shortcuts to pleasure and happiness are also rinsed from us. We leave the book having left pretence behind, and dwell in the loving presence of the Creator.

What do you want to take with you from your study of Ecclesiastes?

MICHAEL MITTON

Farming in the Bible

The books of the Old and New Testament have their roots firmly in the soil. Few of the Old Testament characters we know so well were city dwellers and, even for those who were, cities then were so small that it was impossible to be unaware of the surrounding countryside. The parables of Christ, too, use images taken from farming practices, their wisdom illustrated by the rhythms of planting and reaping.

Agricultural practices changed during the time the Bible was written. The nation left its nomadic lifestyle and settled in 'a land flowing with milk and honey' (Exodus 3:8). Successful farming depended on the covenant relationship with God. Fertility was considered to be allied to trust in God and obedience to his word. Farming practices, linked to spiritual and moral values, included high standards of land management and animal welfare. The land was to be left fallow every seventh year. The conditions for successful food production, fertile land, water and the seasons were understood as God's gift to humanity.

By the time of Solomon, food production had prospered to such an extent that many agricultural products were exported. Increasing wealth, however, brought social inequalities as people exploited the land for profit. The scriptures, however, consistently emphasised that land was gifted by God, for the benefit of all. Every 50th year—designated a year of jubilee—possession of the land was to be restored to its original tribal owners (Leviticus 25:23–28).

Religious festivals were important to the agricultural year, too, and often aligned with other events in the life of the nation. Passover, using unleavened bread, occurred at the beginning of the barley harvest. Some 50 days later, the Festival of Weeks was celebrated, with the offering of the first fruits of the wheat harvest. The Feast of Tabernacles or Booths was the festival of ingathering that took place when the harvest had been completed.

This short introduction to farming in the Bible gives some background to the stories that mean so much to us. With increased knowledge of these practices and the reasons behind them, a greater insight into the meanings of the passages can be gained.

NICK READ

33

Humankind's vocation

And the Lord God planted a garden in Eden, in the east; and there he put the man whom he had formed. Out of the ground the Lord God made to grow every tree that is pleasant to the sight and good for food, the tree of life also in the midst of the garden, and the tree of the knowledge of good and evil... The Lord God took the man and put him in the garden of Eden to till it and keep it. And the Lord God commanded the man, 'You may freely eat of every tree of the garden; but of the tree of the knowledge of good and evil you shall not eat, for in the day that you eat of it you shall die.'

In the scriptures, agriculture is considered to be the primary human activity. The original task of human beings was for them to be the ones who tilled the ground and kept it. The Hebrew word for 'cultivate' or 'till' (*avad*) also meant 'to work' and 'to serve'. From this root come words such as 'servant', 'work' and 'worship'. Working the ground, therefore, was part of humanity's blessing from God. The word translated as 'keep' (*shamar*) included the idea of a protection or a covering, to watch over something. It is the word used in Numbers 6:24: 'The Lord bless you and keep you.' Humankind was to be responsible for the land and protect it.

Of course, the story did not end there. Within the garden was the tree with forbidden fruit. This was not required for either food or happiness, and eating it affected our relationship with God and with the earth: 'Cursed is the ground because of you; in toil you shall eat of it all the days of your life; thorns and thistles it shall bring forth for you; and you shall eat the plants of the field' (Genesis 3:17–18). Nevertheless, the original purpose of human existence remains the same; good farming demands that we serve the land, watch over and keep it.

A true conservationist is a man who knows that the world is not given by his fathers, but borrowed from his children.

Attributed to John James Audubon

NICK READ

Our bond with the soil

Then the Lord God formed man from the dust of the ground, and breathed into his nostrils the breath of life; and the man became a living being. And the Lord God planted a garden in Eden, in the east; and there he put the man whom he had formed... 'By the sweat of your face you shall eat bread until you return to the ground, for out of it you were taken; you are dust, and to dust you shall return.'

Scriptural insight has always stressed the importance of our relationship with the soil. It is a much deeper insight than simply being dependent on fertile soil for food production; it is understood as a fundamental relationship that defines what it means to be human. The Hebrew love of wordplay provides a clue. *Adam* is the Hebrew word for 'man', which is related to *adamah*, the Hebrew word for dust from the ground. Human beings and soil are interconnected. If wordplay does not convince you, the link becomes explicit in Genesis 3, particularly verse 19: 'you are dust, and to dust you shall return.' If our original vocation was to till and keep the land (Genesis 2:15), it was given to us on the clear understanding that we are fundamentally connected to this life-giving resource.

In 2015, the journal *Science* contained a report that global soil fertility has reached its peak and is likely to decline within the foreseeable future. Within the same period it is estimated that the world's population will rise from 6.8 billion to 9 billion. Technology has helped to improve yields by developments in plant breeding, pesticides and herbicides, but caring for the soil remains the key to our future well-being. We have a responsibility, not just for ourselves but also for the entire world and the generations that will inhabit this world after us, to care for the ground beneath our feet.

Lord God, we give you thanks for the life-giving soil. Give us grace to cherish, nourish and protect our common heritage. Amen
(If possible, say this prayer while holding a handful of soil.)

NICK READ

Land

You shall observe my statutes... so that you may live on the land securely... The land shall not be sold in perpetuity, for the land is mine; with me you are but aliens and tenants. Throughout the land that you hold, you shall provide for the redemption of the land. If anyone of your kin falls into difficulty and sells a piece of property, then the next-of-kin shall come and redeem what the relative has sold.

The year of jubilee in Leviticus 25, as noted earlier, occurred every 50 years. Any land that had been sold reverted to its original owner. Because all land was held in trust, as it came from God, ownership was understood to be communal. Land was allocated to tribes and families in accordance with need. It was each family's responsibility to redeem land that had been sold, thus retaining the means to secure food and livelihood for future generations.

One of the most contentious issues of justice in world agriculture today is access to land, as peasant farmers are disinherited and forced to seek employment in urban areas. In the UK, private ownership is the norm and the proportion of tenanted land is comparatively small. Many agricultural tenancies are relatively short-term. Within the next decade, the Royal Agricultural Society estimates that 60,000 new entrants will be required to manage UK farms, and many of these 'new entrants' will not be able to raise the capital required to buy land or equipment.

One response has been a growth in community initiatives, such as allotments, city farms, guerrilla gardening and community orchards. They are important opportunities to try alternative agricultural systems, enable new entrants to get started, promote artisan businesses and develop local food chains. We can join in with these initiatives, either through active participation or thoughtful purchasing.

The spirit of the Jubilee urges us to cry 'Enough!' to the many... intolerable situations of dire poverty and injustice. We must call attention to the special and essential significance of justice in the biblical message—that of protection of the weak and of their right, as children of God, to the wealth of creation.

Pontifical Council for Justice and Peace

NICK READ

Fallow

The Lord spoke to Moses on Mount Sinai, saying: Speak to the people of Israel and say to them: When you enter the land that I am giving you, the land shall observe a sabbath for the Lord. For six years you shall sow your field, and for six years you shall prune your vineyard, and gather in their yield; but in the seventh year there shall be a sabbath of complete rest for the land, a sabbath for the Lord; you shall not sow your field or prune your vineyard. You shall not reap the aftergrowth of your harvest or gather the grapes of your unpruned vine: it shall be a year of complete rest for the land. You may eat what the land yields during its sabbath—you, your male and female slaves, your hired and your bound labourers who live with you; for your livestock also, and for the wild animals in your land all its yield shall be for food.

Many commentators rightly emphasise the beneficial effect that resting the land every seventh year would have. A fallow year allows the soil to recover its fertility, but what about the effects on the farmer? Within an agrarian community, the seventh year of rest for field and vineyard also means that the farmer must cease from sowing or pruning. His welfare, and those for whom he is responsible, remains assured as food is still available, but what does he do if he is not farming?

One of the issues faced by agricultural chaplains is the growing number of farmers in their 70s or 80s who should have retired, but have not or cannot. They struggle with the physical and emotional demands of the job, yet their lives are so bound with farming that they cannot conceive of living without it. While it is a genuine source of pride to be a good farmer, it can be catastrophic when people reach the point where they believe that their worth lies solely in terms of what they do.

---

*O Lord, give us grace to embrace fallow times and remember that
our worth lies in our relationship with you, not in our work
or achievements. Amen*

NICK READ

Blessing and judgement

O children of Zion, be glad and rejoice in the Lord your God; for he has given the early rain for your vindication, he has poured down for you abundant rain, the early and the later rain, as before. The threshing-floors shall be full of grain, the vats shall overflow with wine and oil. I will repay you for the years that the swarming locust has eaten, the hopper, the destroyer, and the cutter, my great army, which I sent against you. You shall eat in plenty and be satisfied, and praise the name of the Lord your God, who has dealt wondrously with you. And my people shall never again be put to shame.

In the lands written about in the Bible, light early rains commenced in late October and fell for up to two months. Heavier winter rains fell from December to March. Late rains occurred in March and April. Early rains were essential for effective germination, while the late rains swelled the grain coming to maturity before harvest. The provision of timely rain was viewed as a blessing from God.

The greatest danger to crops was locusts. A swarm of desert locusts contained millions of insects covering several square kilometres of land. They devastated the farms affected, eating all plants, yet neigh-bouring farms might be completely untouched as the locusts' path was largely determined by the prevailing wind. Their destructive power was seen as a judgement from God.

Today, too, severe weather conditions regularly affect harvests, endangering the livelihoods of farmers. Major outbreaks of disease, such as Foot and Mouth, can devastate entire communities. Good farming practices and the support of the local and international community protect and aid those caught up in such misfortunes.

O most merciful Father, who of thy gracious goodness hast heard the devout prayers of thy Church, and turned our dearth and scarcity into cheapness and plenty: We give thee humble thanks for this thy special bounty; beseeching thee to continue thy loving-kindness unto us, that our land may yield us her fruits of increase, to thy glory and comfort; through Jesus Christ our Lord. Amen

'Thanksgiving for Plenty', The Book of Common Prayer

NICK READ

Justice and the food economy

When you reap the harvest of your land, you shall not reap to the very edges of your field, or gather the gleanings of your harvest. You shall not strip your vineyard bare, or gather the fallen grapes of your vineyard; you shall leave them for the poor and for the alien. I am the Lord your God. You shall not steal; you shall not deal falsely; and you shall not lie to one another.

It seems a strange juxtaposition—the practical injunctions about harvesting next to instructions about honesty and truthfulness—but the writers of Leviticus made no distinction between how they farmed and how they should live as a community. At the heart of the passage is a concern for others and an understanding that what is done should be for the benefit of all.

The way that we produce food today should also not prejudice others or prevent them from benefiting from God's providence. It is a dilemma for modern agri-business, its restrictive practices often seeming to run counter to these basic principles. The cost of producing basic foodstuffs remains critical for the economy and may vary according to world supply, affecting the price that is paid to the producer. Such variation can be increased by large supermarket consortiums. Eager to attract shoppers, they may force producers to lower their prices. Low prices benefit consumers, but can endanger the livelihoods of farmers, who must work ever harder for less profit.

Are ever-cheaper goods the only criteria that matter in a modern food economy? The power of the individual to affect the way farmers are treated should not be underestimated. We must be prepared to pay more for our basic foodstuffs so that others, in turn, may eat.

The Fairtrade movement started to protect producers in developing countries. It sought better prices, decent working conditions, local sustainability and fair terms of trade for farmers and workers. It required companies to pay sustainable prices (which should never fall lower than the market price). Should this approach not apply everywhere?

NICK READ

Moral concerns

If you follow my decrees and are careful to obey my commands, I will send you the seasonal rains. The land will then yield its crops, and the trees of the field will produce their fruit. Your threshing season will overlap with the grape harvest, and your grape harvest will overlap with the season of planting grain. You will eat your fill and live securely in your own land.

The ability to farm well is closely linked to and conditional on God's covenant promises. The moral universe and natural world are interwoven. Faithful obedience to God brings the blessing of seasonal rains, leading to abundance. Modern agriculture is a technologically advanced industry at the cutting edge of science. Machinery has significantly replaced human labour; geographic information systems (GIS) are commonplace in modern tractors and combines; genetically modified (GM) food and plant and animal breeding have led to higher yields and greater disease resistance, and the use of chemicals in fertilisers, pesticides and veterinary products is commonplace.

None of these advances removes the need for moral choice. If anything, they intensify the moral dilemmas associated with farming. Scientific research centres today spend a significant proportion of their budgets on protecting GM crops from anti-GM protesters; communities oppose large-scale poultry or dairy units; religious leaders are asked to determine whether or not eating the flesh of a cow that has had genes from a pig inserted into its DNA violates food laws. The family farm today therefore remains at the cutting edge of moral enquiry.

Where does the moral responsibility begin and end? Most of us do not farm and we may not understand, in detail, the science or technologies involved, but we all consume. We are the market, so all of us have a responsibility to uphold the relationship between farming and the covenant promise by being interested in how our food is produced. We should ask questions and, if necessary, challenge or change our habits.

Thank you for our food, but in its abundance please do not allow any of us to become complacent about how our food is produced. Amen

NICK READ

Good husbandry

Know well the condition of your flocks, and give attention to your herds; for riches do not last for ever, nor a crown for all generations. When the grass is gone, and new growth appears, and the herbage of the mountains is gathered, the lambs will provide your clothing, and the goats the price of a field; there will be enough goats' milk for your food, for the food of your household and nourishment for your servant-girls.

Good farming involves intimate relationships between people and soil, people and animals and, as the passage reminds us, people and God. Animal husbandry—the care and management of flocks and herds—is often described as an 'art'. The traditional picture of the shepherd or stockman is of one who knows his animals, is able to diagnose problems and works to enhance their welfare.

Technology has an impact on modern farming. Genomics is the science that helps to identify the genetic potential of an animal so that it can be selected for breeding on the basis of the traits it is expected to show. Conventional selection takes longer as the animal can only be evaluated after its progeny have been born and have grown up. This can take over five years from the birth of a dairy bull, as the bull's offspring need to have their own calves, to start giving milk, before the true value of the breeding can be determined.

Technology does not alter the fundamentals of good husbandry, however. Looking after animals still requires local knowledge and attention to detail. Every farm is different and within each farm every field offers a unique environment. Every herd is different and within each herd each animal remains unique. It is only by understanding such intimate details that farming realises its full potential.

The Bible uses the language of animal husbandry to refer to the relationship between God and us: 'Know that the Lord is God. It is he that made us, and we are his; we are his people, and the sheep of his pasture' (Psalm 100:3). As members of his flock, each of us is unique, known by God and having his undivided attention.

NICK READ

Animal welfare

When you come upon your enemy's ox or donkey going astray, you shall bring it back. When you see the donkey of one who hates you lying under its burden and you would hold back from setting it free, you must help to set it free... For six days you shall do your work, but on the seventh day you shall rest, so that your ox and your donkey may have relief, and your home-born slave and the resident alien may be refreshed. Be attentive to all that I have said to you.

The scriptures respect non-human life as a fundamental principle. Proverbs defines the righteous person as one who cares for his or her animals (Proverbs 12:10). Throughout the Old Testament, laws stipulating high welfare standards for farm animals are set out. These include the injunction not to muzzle an ox while it is threshing grain (Deuteronomy 25:4). The basis for these standards is often over-looked, however: it's not that the animals are considered important to us, but that they are important to God.

Animals used for farming were included within the provisions of God's covenant with Israel. The justification for the sabbath rest given in Exodus 23:12 is that human beings should rest so that they can provide relief for their beasts of burden. The animals are not incidental to the sabbath but are highlighted as the beneficiaries. Through his law, God demonstrates his concern for the welfare of these creatures. It was not a question of ownership: if the animal did not belong to you, or even if it belonged to your enemy, the same principles applied. Animal charities today continue this attitude of concern for every creature—an approach we can all live by.

The earth is the Lord's and the fullness thereof. O God, enlarge within us the sense of fellowship with all living things, even our brothers, the animals, to whom thou gavest the earth as their home in common with us... May we realise that they live, not for us alone, but for themselves and for thee and that they love the sweetness of life. Amen

Attributed to St Basil

NICK READ

Environmental guardianship

As for you, my flock, thus says the Lord God: I shall judge between sheep and sheep, between ram and goats. Is it not enough for you to feed on the good pasture, but you must tread down with your feet the rest of your pasture? When you drink of clear water, must you foul the rest with your feet? And must my sheep eat what you have trodden with your feet, and drink what you have fouled with your feet?

Ezekiel was not writing principally about environmental steward-ship. The oracle was a condemnation of the 'shepherds' of Israel for their selfishness. They had so much, but their greed and lack of concern prevented others from benefiting even from what was left. Nevertheless, this passage is a remarkably astute observation regard-ing the current debate about farming and the environment.

Water and soil loss from agricultural land carries heavy penalties for natural ecosystems. Nutrients that are essential for healthy crops can be serious pollutants if they enter fresh water. Nitrate vulnerable zones (NVZs) were designated to restrict the quantities and timing of nitro-gen fertiliser and manures being used on agricultural land in order to reduce leaching into streams and lakes. Similar measures apply in some areas for phosphates. The Rivers Trust—a charity that acts to protect river environments—has been working with farmers to fence off river-banks so that cattle do not poach (tread) the soil on the riverbank, leading to soil erosion.

These activities come at a price, to both the farmer and the taxpayer, so can be contentious. When money is scarce, the environment often comes low in the pecking order of priorities, but a healthy environ-ment is not an optional extra. Rather, it is a fundamental requirement of life. Further, there is a divine imperative. Ezekiel understood the effects that farming practices could have on environmental health, and the importance of environmental health to the well-being of all.

Lord, grant us wisdom to care for the earth. Help us to act now for the good of future generations and all your creatures. Help us to become instruments of a new creation, founded on the covenant of your love.

NICK READ

Slaughter

If your gift for a burnt-offering is from the flock, from the sheep or goats, your offering shall be a male without blemish. It shall be slaughtered on the north side of the altar before the Lord, and Aaron's sons the priests shall dash its blood against all sides of the altar. It shall be cut up into its parts, with its head and its suet, and the priest shall arrange them on the wood that is on the fire of the altar; but the entrails and the legs shall be washed with water. Then the priest shall offer the whole and turn it into smoke on the altar; it is a burnt-offering, an offering by fire of pleasing odour to the Lord.

Unless vegetarian, no agricultural community could avoid taking an animal's life, whether for food or skin. At the heart of the Old Testament is a fundamental principle: all life is sacred, whether human or animal.

Leviticus draws no distinction between slaughtering an animal for food and making a sacrifice to God (although Deuteronomy 12:15 does). In Leviticus, all animals slaughtered for food are also to be offered as sacrifice. In practice, therefore, the farmer brought the animal to be killed and was responsible for its death. The priest took the requisite portions of the animal to be offered to God and put them on the altar. The family were permitted to eat what remained as their food.

As the animal's life belonged to God, signified by the blood, no human was ever permitted to eat the blood of a slaughtered animal: 'For the life of the flesh is in the blood' (Leviticus 17:11). Instead, the blood had to be returned to God via the altar or sprinkled on the ground. Killing an animal for food was permissible, but slaughtering the animal was to be carried out before God as part of the covenant relationship.

Freud wrote about the 'sacred meal', found in many religions—the idea of sharing a meal with God. Holy Communion is a particular understanding of this, but, in the Old Testament, preparing and eating food is always considered holy.

NICK READ

Partnering God

The Lord spoke to Moses: Speak to the people of Israel and say to them: When you enter the land that I am giving you and you reap its harvest, you shall bring the sheaf of the first fruits of your harvest to the priest. He shall raise the sheaf before the Lord, so that you may find acceptance; on the day after the sabbath the priest shall raise it... You shall observe the festival of harvest, of the first fruits of your labour, of what you sow in the field. You shall observe the festival of ingathering at the end of the year, when you gather in from the field the fruit of your labour.

The festivals associated with harvest are not only about its successful conclusion. God's help is invoked at every step. Our modern harvest festivals are largely derived from the actions of an eccentric Victorian Cornishman, the Revd Robert Hawker of Morwenstow, who wanted to help his rural parish celebrate the agricultural year. His ideas were gradually adopted throughout the country. Our harvest festivals today tend to focus on our wheat harvest in September/October. This is changing and areas where livestock farming is more prevalent may celebrate harvest with a 'lamb service' in spring. Similarly, Apple Day has become a national event, associated with the cider industry. Plough Sunday and Rogation Days remain in the church calendar, when God's blessing is asked for tilling, sowing and the harvest.

The scriptural tradition constantly reminds us of the significance of the partnership between God and man throughout the whole agricultural cycle, not just giving thanks at the end. Bringing the sheaf of the first fruits was in order to invoke God's blessing and gain his acceptance. It acknowledged that the crucial weeks to come, when the rest of the harvest still had to be gathered, also required God and man to work together if it was to be successful.

Although we have goals to aspire to and measures of success, everything we do, every day, happens in partnership with God. The first fruits are as important as the final ingathering. Each is a cause for celebration and an exercise in holiness.

NICK READ

God is like the farmer

Listen, and hear my voice; Pay attention, and hear my speech. Do those who plough for sowing plough continually? Do they continually open and harrow their ground? When they have levelled its surface, do they not scatter dill, sow cummin, and plant wheat in rows and barley in its proper place, and spelt as the border? For they are well instructed; their God teaches them. Dill is not threshed with a threshing-sledge, nor is a cartwheel rolled over cummin; but dill is beaten out with a stick, and cummin with a rod. Grain is crushed for bread, but one does not thresh it for ever; one drives the cartwheel and horses over it, but does not pulverise it. This also comes from the Lord of hosts; he is wonderful in counsel, and excellent in wisdom.

Isaiah believed that the age-old wisdom of agriculture, which preceded written history, was a gift imparted by God. His parable asks whether certain farming activities, such as ploughing, harrowing, sowing and threshing, occur all the time or are time-dependent. The answer, of course, is that they are time-dependent. He also noted that the techniques of threshing (separating the edible grain from chaff) were specific to each crop. Using the wrong technique would destroy the harvested seed rather than enable it to be used as food. The four crops mentioned—dill, cumin, wheat and barley—were familiar to the small farming communities of Judah.

Isaiah deduced that God was like the farmer. He dealt with his people appropriately according to their situation. There was a time for judgement and punishment, but there was also a time for healing and restoration. Isaiah uses the two most destructive farming activities—ploughing, which breaks up the soil, and crushing, to make flour—as analogies for judgement. But they were coming to an end. Although the grain may be crushed, it is not pulverised.

Whether today is for ploughing, harrowing, sowing or threshing, please let me remember that I spend it with the Lord of hosts, wonderful in counsel and excellent in wisdom. Amen

NICK READ

The good shepherd

'The one who enters by the gate is the shepherd of the sheep. The gatekeeper opens the gate for him, and the sheep hear his voice. He calls his own sheep by name and leads them out. When he has brought out all his own, he goes ahead of them, and the sheep follow him because they know his voice. They will not follow a stranger, but they will run from him because they do not know the voice of strangers... I am the good shepherd. The good shepherd lays down his life for the sheep. The hired hand, who is not the shepherd and does not own the sheep, sees the wolf coming and leaves the sheep and runs away—and the wolf scatters them and snatches them. The hired hand runs away because a hired hand does not care for the sheep. I am the good shepherd.'

Flocks in Israel were not driven from behind, but led by their shepherds, each using a unique call. Each flock would learn to recognise the voice of its shepherd and his call. At night, all flocks were corralled together in the communal village sheepfold. One shepherd would stand watch to protect them from predators and thieves and the other shepherds would go to their homes. Any thief, of course, would avoid the gate where the watchman was located and enter by climbing over the wall. The following morning, the shepherds would return and, after being recognised by the night watchman, would enter the fold to call out their flock and lead them to fresh pasture.

Based on this farming scene, Jesus tells truths about himself. His is the authentic voice of God and his flock will recognise his voice. He is the true shepherd, rather than a hired hand who does not care for the welfare of the flock. It is a story of the familiarity between Jesus and his followers. It also speaks of God protecting his people. It was the shepherd's job to protect the flock, to put his own life on the line for the sheep's welfare.

'I am the good shepherd. The good shepherd lays down his life
for the sheep' (John 10:11).

NICK READ

The Songs of Ascent

For the next fortnight we shall be reflecting on a fascinating group of psalms known as the Songs of Ascent (Psalms 120—134). It is usually assumed that they were sung by groups of pilgrims to Jerusalem as they made their way up the final slopes towards their great objective—the magnificent temple of the Lord. It was the ambition of every Jew, no matter where they lived, to visit the temple, and they often formed a party to make the long journey together. It was customary for pilgrims to be offered hospitality at each stopping place—food, drink and a place to spread out their mattresses for the night. From Nazareth to Jerusalem, for instance, was 60 miles. With older members in a party, as well as children and infants, ten or twelve miles a day would be good going, so the journey could take days, or even weeks, to make. No wonder, when they got near, they wanted to sing!

There are several things to bear in mind when reading these psalms. The first is that they are poetry. The second is that they were meant to be sung. The third is that they were written both for worship in the temple and for personal devotion.

The fact that they are poetry should affect the way we read them. We do not usually turn to poems for information, but for inspiration, to be moved rather than informed. The writers of the psalms are prepared to open to us their deepest feelings—of regret, longing, gratitude, repentance and even indignation. Hebrew poetry does not use rhyme or the rhythms of speech, but derives its shape from the balancing of ideas. Each statement will be matched by another, either the same thing expressed differently or, sometimes, a contrary view. The poetic impact is in either their repetition or their contrast. You will find many examples in these often memorable hymns from three millennia ago.

DAVID WINTER

I am for peace

In my distress I cry to the Lord, that he may answer me: 'Deliver me, O Lord, from lying lips, from a deceitful tongue.'... Woe is me, that I am an alien in Meshech, that I must live among the tents of Kedar. Too long have I had my dwelling among those who hate peace. I am for peace; but when I speak, they are for war.

This does not really sound like a song of excitement and joy at arriving at one's destination! As the first of the 'Songs of Ascent' it sets a sombre tone. After the death of Solomon, Israel and Judah were subjected to constant attacks by their powerful neighbours, often culminating in large numbers of Jewish people being taken off as captives. The background of this song seems to be that of such people—reluctant residents of Mesech, living 'among the tents of Kedar' (v. 5) rather than in the homely setting of the promised land and near the holy city of Jerusalem and its magnificent temple.

After a time, many people taken into captivity became what we would now call 'migrants', living peacefully as aliens in a foreign land. In this case, however, it seems that the 'host community' was resentful of their presence. People said offensive things about them—evident from the phrases 'lying lips' and 'deceitful tongue' (v. 2). The exiles wanted peace, but when they talked of it, the others were for war.

'Peace' is a great word in the Psalms. The Hebrew word for it is *shalom*, which means much more than simply an absence of war. 'Shalom' is wholeness, living at one with our Creator God, with creation and our neighbours. That, however, is difficult if the neighbours prefer confrontation. In such circumstances, unwilling exiles long to be among their kindred, where they believe peace can be found. Jesus said, 'Blessed are the peacemakers' (Matthew 5:9). Notice, though, that peace has to be 'made'. Like the psalmist here, we have to be 'for' peace, then work for it.

Jesus made 'peace through the blood of his cross' (Colossians 1:20). That's a powerful reminder that peace always has a price.

DAVID WINTER

The guard who never sleeps

I lift up my eyes to the hills—from where will my help come? My help comes from the LORD, who made heaven and earth. He will not let your foot be moved; he who keeps you will not slumber. He who keeps Israel will neither slumber nor sleep. The LORD is your keeper; the LORD is your shade at your right hand. The sun shall not strike you by day, nor the moon by night. The LORD will keep you from all evil; he will keep your life. The LORD will keep your going out and your coming in from this time on and for evermore.

Perhaps as the pilgrims neared Jerusalem they were excited by its location, built on a hill and surrounded by hills. They lifted up their eyes to see them and wondered if their 'help' (v. 1) would come from the mountains (as many people in the ancient world believed). So this beautiful psalm is an extended answer to the question, 'From where will my help come?' (v. 1). It is expressed in poetry of memorable power and beauty. Help does not come from the hills or from the plains or anywhere else. It comes from the LORD who created them.

The capital letters for 'LORD' are important, Whenever they are used in our Bibles it means that the word being translated is the holy name of God, Yahweh, 'I AM'—the One who simply exists, who is permanent present tense, who has no beginning or end but is eternal, and is the source of our daily help. That is some promise!

'Help' is a really homespun word used to describe a major attribute of God himself. He is our 'helper' in daily life, stopping us stumbling, protecting us from evil things, shading us from the sun's heat and (as they saw it then) the malign effect of the moon (v. 6). Every time we go out or come in (v. 8), God is with us.

God is our guard who never sleeps, our helper who is always there.

DAVID WINTER

Happy band of pilgrims

I was glad when they said to me, 'Let us go to the house of the Lord!' Our feet are standing within your gates, O Jerusalem. Jerusalem—built as a city that is bound firmly together. To it the tribes go up, the tribes of the Lord, as was decreed for Israel, to give thanks to the name of the Lord... Pray for the peace of Jerusalem: 'May they prosper who love you. Peace be within your walls, and security within your towers.' For the sake of my relatives and friends I will say, 'Peace be within you.' For the sake of the house of the Lord our God, I will seek your good.

At last the pilgrims have reached their goal. Their feet are within the gates of the city of Jerusalem. At any moment, they will enter the magnificent arch into the temple of the Lord. 'I was glad,' says one pilgrim (v. 1), when the idea was first mooted of going up to the house of the Lord. Then it was an idea. Now it is a reality! The note of wonder and joy is infectious: 'We have made it, we are here!'

Then it seems as if someone else speaks, maybe the party leader. Rather like a tour guide, he points out a few facts: the compact nature of the city, the decree that all true Israelites, from all the tribes, should make their way there to worship the Lord.

Perhaps it is yet another person who speaks next, possibly a rabbi who has travelled with them. He calls them as they stand there, awe-struck, to turn to prayer. The first petition is for the peace of Jerusalem. How often, how constantly all through history, has that prayer been needed—as it is today? Peace and security have, over the long centuries, evaded this great city, the birthplace of our faith.

Then the invitation, as they stand there, is to pray for their 'relatives and friends'—the people they have left behind in their distant villages. May they know peace, too. Then, the final topic for prayer, now visible before them, is what Jews called 'the house of the Lord our God' (v. 9).

'I was glad!' We may know the dramatic choral setting of those words, but are we glad? Do our hearts lift up with joy at the very thought of gathering with others to worship?

DAVID WINTER

A servant's prayer

To you I lift up my eyes, O you who are enthroned in the heavens! As the eyes of servants look to the hand of their master, as the eyes of a maid to the hand of her mistress, so our eyes look to the Lord our God, until he has mercy upon us. Have mercy upon us, O Lord, have mercy upon us, for we have had more than enough of contempt. Our soul has had more than its fill of the scorn of those who are at ease, of the contempt of the proud.

Slaves were part of the ancient world. Some were treated simply as being there to do their owners' bidding. Others (and there are many examples in the Bible) were trusted members of their households, genuinely loved. Remember the slave of the centurion whom he begged Jesus to heal? Paul did say that 'in Christ' there is 'neither bond nor free', but even he urged Christian slaves to be good servants to their masters.

This psalm offers two images of that service: the male servant watching the hand of his master and the female slave watching her mistress' hand. What they were to be alert to was a sign of command. Obedience had to be instant, so they had to be constantly watching and waiting.

That was how the psalmist saw the role of the servants of the Lord, too. We are to watch (that is, be attentive to his purposes) and wait (that is, to carry out his promptings). Our heavenly master is not cruel or unthinking. He loves his servants and values them. His service (literally, slavery) is perfect freedom.

The last part of this psalm is a reminder of how down-to-earth and honest these hymns of worship are. Sometimes this is how we feel. We have had enough of being treated like dirt by people who have some kind of power over us. So the psalmist simply tells God, with a plea that he will mercifully deliver them.

The apostle Paul often described himself as the slave (doulos) of Jesus Christ. That 'slavery', of course, was a voluntary submission to the wise and gentle rule of love.

DAVID WINTER

The God who is on our side

If it had not been the Lord who was on our side—let Israel now say—if it had not been the Lord who was on our side, when our enemies attacked us, then they would have swallowed us up alive, when their anger was kindled against us; then the flood would have swept us away, the torrent would have gone over us; then over us would have gone the raging waters… Our help is in the name of the Lord, who made heaven and earth.

As a group of friends on a journey to a place of pilgrimage reflect on the experience, it is not unexpected that they think about the past as well as the present. So, here, their song is not about the glory ahead—when they will worship God in the glorious temple—but the way in which God has been with them in the past. This is, in fact, a recital of past events, moments when things looked black (when they would have been 'swallowed… up alive', v. 3) but then the God they worship intervened. They rehearse various experiences of deliverance—from enemies, floods, raging torrents. Whomever and whatever was against them, their testimony is that God was for them, 'on our side' (v. 1).

That is a wonderful truth. Matthew's Gospel says that Jesus is to be called 'Emmanuel'—a title given to the Messiah in a prophecy in Isaiah (Isaiah 7:14; Matthew 1:23). 'Emmanuel' is usually translated as 'God with us', but, equally, it means 'God for us' or, as here, 'God on our side'. It is a truly transformative moment to think of the creator of the universe as being 'on our side'. Too many people see God as a kind of opponent, making things difficult and complicated. In fact, as Paul said, 'If God is for us, who is against us?' (Romans 8:31).

There is no bypass avoiding the troubles of life, but the maker of heaven and earth is 'on our side': 'You are with me; your rod and staff—they comfort me' (Psalm 23:4).

DAVID WINTER

Surrounded by the Lord

Those who trust in the Lord are like Mount Zion, which cannot be moved, but abides for ever. As the mountains surround Jerusalem, so the Lord surrounds his people, from this time on and for evermore. For the sceptre of wickedness shall not rest on the land allotted to the righteous, so that the righteous may not stretch out their hands to do wrong. Do good, O Lord, to those who are good, and to those who are upright in their hearts. But those who turn aside to their own crooked ways the Lord will lead away with evildoers. Peace be upon Israel!

It seems that the pilgrims have reached Jerusalem and are struck—as any visitors are—by its impressive location. It stands on a mountain, Zion, but it is also surrounded by mountains and hills. It feels like a natural fortress, secure among the everlasting heights. So, they reflect that just as the mountains surround the city of Jerusalem, like silent watchful guards, so the Lord surrounds his people for ever.

As they stood there, the 'city of God' probably seemed impregnable. It was not, of course, as history was soon to show, but they found the impression that its position created helpful and reassuring.

The rest of the psalm takes a different tack. Like most of the psalms in this group, it is concerned with the difference between the 'righteous' and the 'wicked'. Wickedness, they felt, could never hold sway in the city of God. Surely the inhabitants of this holy place would never 'stretch out their hands to do wrong' (v. 3)? Well, of course they would, and did, because even holy places are occupied by sinners, like everywhere else. The Lord, they asserted, would reward the righteous and upright and 'lead away' (v. 5) the evildoers. This is in one sense absolutely true. God's judgement is unavoidable. It took the coming of the Messiah, his Son, to declare, 'I have come to call not the righteous but sinners' (Mark 2:17).

Jesus the Messiah died on the cross for sinners, but that includes those described here as 'righteous', because 'there is no one who is righteous, not even one' (Romans 3:10).

DAVID WINTER

Sowing in tears, reaping in joy

When the Lord restored the fortunes of Zion, we were like those who dream. Then our mouth was filled with laughter, and our tongue with shouts of joy; then it was said among the nations, 'The Lord has done great things for them.' The Lord has done great things for us, and we rejoiced. Restore our fortunes, O Lord, like the watercourses in the Negeb. May those who sow in tears reap with shouts of joy. Those who go out weeping, bearing the seed for sowing, shall come home with shouts of joy, carrying their sheaves.

This psalm can be enjoyed and appreciated at many levels. As a poem, it is a gem. The echoing of the phrases expresses the emotions of the singers. As someone who, like most people, has experienced moments of sowing in tears (v. 5), I can respond to its wonderfully positive message. As a song of praise, it lifts up the heart. It captures a kaleidoscope of human emotions in a setting of glorious thanksgiving. Go on, read it again… and again! It is worth it.

It would seem that the singers are older people who can remember the dark days before David 'restored the fortunes' of Israel (v. 1). Coming out of those days was a wonderful and liberating experience. Even foreigners recognised it: 'The Lord has done great things for them' (v. 2).

The song then becomes a prayer for continued blessing. The pilgrims compare their needs now to the dry lands of the Negeb, which are suddenly nourished as its water courses fill up and the crops begin to flourish. That thought leads us into the most profound part of the psalm—the whole notion of blessing coming out of pain. Those who sow in tears—bereavement, perhaps—may eventually reap with joy (v. 5). Those who go out weeping, but 'bearing the seed for sowing' (that is, with faith in God's ultimate purposes), will come home 'carrying their sheaves' (v. 6).

Both sorrow and joy produce tears. We should not reject either experience.

DAVID WINTER

Priorities and values

Unless the Lord builds the house, those who build it labour in vain. Unless the Lord guards the city, the guard keeps watch in vain. It is in vain that you rise up early and go late to rest, eating the bread of anxious toil; for he gives sleep to his beloved. Sons are indeed a heritage from the Lord, the fruit of the womb a reward. Like arrows in the hand of a warrior are the sons of one's youth.

This, perhaps more than any of the other psalms in this group, is a message for the Western world in the 21st century. If people built selfishly 3000 years ago, today some people own many houses while others struggle even to find a couple of rooms in which to raise their families. We are obsessed with security, yet feel constantly insecure. For many people, daily work is indeed 'anxious toil' (v. 2), involving an early start to catch a train or bus, and the working day extending into the evening. At the same time, many people long for regular work and despair of finding it. We work for our daily bread, but sometimes are so stressed that we cannot enjoy it when it is on the table. Then our sleep is disturbed by anxious thoughts and cares, so that the Creator's loving gift of sleep is denied us.

That is, of course, a pessimistic view of daily life! The psalmist does offer a remedy, though: 'Unless the Lord builds the house…' (v. 1). What if he does? Suppose, in the hectic world of work, we see the hand of God guiding us? What if our priority is not success, but serenity? Can we recognise that the only true security is in the guardianship of God?

This psalm is certainly robust in its analysis of human priorities and values, but it is also positive in its words of assurance. If the Lord builds the house, we have a true home. If the Lord guards the city, we are truly secure. If the Lord gives purpose to toil, we can sleep in peace. The psalmist's final thought is that the house becomes a home, where children are valued and loved.

We live in a world of rush and stress, where sleeping pills often replace a night-time prayer. Changing our priorities might help to create a more peaceful, sane and secure way of life.

DAVID WINTER

Bless this house!

Happy is everyone who fears the Lord, who walks in his ways. You shall eat the fruit of the labour of your hands; you shall be happy, and it shall go well with you. Your wife will be like a fruitful vine within your house; your children will be like olive shoots around your table. Thus shall the man be blessed who fears the Lord. The Lord bless you from Zion. May you see the prosperity of Jerusalem all the days of your life. May you see your children's children. Peace be upon Israel!

This psalm neatly balances the message of the previous one. Psalm 127 warned of the danger of a home life not based on reverence for God and his purposes, while this one speaks of the blessings of the home that is. 'Fearing' the Lord does not mean being terrified by the very thought of him. He is, after all, 'our Father'. It simply means having 'reverence'. The opening words of the Lord's Prayer express the paradox exactly: 'Our Father in heaven, hallowed be your name'. We can, in the deepest way, respect and honour those we love.

In a household run on godly principles, there will be food on the table ('the fruit of the labour of your hands', v. 2) and happiness around it. I love the image of the children 'like olive shoots' (v. 3) as they tuck into a meal! The wife, in line with the thinking of the time, is primarily seen in terms of reproduction. Here she is 'a fruitful vine' (v. 3)—laden not only with olive shoots but also grapes. The psalmist and the singers making their way to the great city of God offer a blessing 'from Zion' (v. 5) on the families they know, together with a prayer that they too may see 'the prosperity of Jerusalem' (v. 5) one day.

The final petition is that their friends may see their 'children's children' (v. 6). I suppose we all hope to see our grandchildren (or grand-nephews and nieces) and, nowadays, most people do. At a time when the average life expectancy was around 50, however, it was something of a privilege to do so. We should count our blessings!

Faith, family, friends—the three great 'F's'.
Take time to give thanks for them.

DAVID WINTER

Gratitude and bitterness

'Often have they attacked me from my youth'—let Israel now say—
'often have they attacked me from my youth, yet they have not
prevailed against me. Those who plough ploughed on my back; they
made their furrows long.' The Lord is righteous; he has cut the cords
of the wicked. May all who hate Zion be put to shame and turned back.
Let them be like the grass on the housetops that withers before it
grows up, with which reapers do not fill their hands or binders of
sheaves their arms.

Perhaps as the pilgrims near Jerusalem an older voice speaks up, saying, 'It was not always like this. In my young days we suffered at the
hands of Israel's enemies. People were taken away as slaves. I was
beaten by enemy soldiers. Yet, whatever our enemies did, the Lord
was still with us, and they were defeated.' His words are then turned
into a prayer: 'May the enemies of Zion, the holy city, be put to shame
and turned back. Indeed, let them be burnt up like the grass on
housetops.' Such bitter words are a reminder of a feature of the Psalms
that often worries modern readers—the invocation of vengeance.

How should Christians read such words? Well, first of all, as utterly
honest. This is how the psalmist felt and he simply told God about it.
I remember long ago visiting a woman whose husband had died of a
sudden heart attack during the night. She launched herself at me,
shouting, 'I hate God!' Months later she came to talk to me, shocked at
what she had said that morning. I assured her that her heavenly Father
knew how she felt and shared her pain.

The Hebrew scriptures are full of God's forgiveness of his people,
but there is very little about our forgiveness of others. The law of
Moses was concerned with limiting vengeance rather than urging forgiveness: 'eye for eye' (Exodus 21:24). It was not until the Messiah
came that we heard a different message: 'If anyone strikes you on the
right cheek, turn the other also' and 'Love your enemies' (Matthew
5:39, 44).

Forgive us our sins, as we forgive those who sin against us.

The Lord's Prayer

DAVID WINTER

Waiting for the Lord

Out of the depths I cry to you, O Lord. Lord, hear my voice! Let your ears be attentive to the voice of my supplications! If you, O Lord, should mark iniquities, Lord, who could stand? But there is forgiveness with you, so that you may be revered. I wait for the Lord, my soul waits, and in his word I hope; my soul waits for the Lord more than those who watch for the morning, more than those who watch for the morning.

It is not surprising that, approaching the awesome temple of God, some of the pilgrims become aware of their own sins, wondering if they are fit to enter the holy courts and make their prayers. In the light of yesterday's psalm, the contrast is quite striking. Then it was the sins of the 'enemy'. Now it is our own sins, which, I suppose, should always be our first priority. No one could 'stand' in worship before the Lord God if the qualification were moral perfection, but 'there is forgiveness with you' (v. 4). It is only on the grounds of God's grace and forgiveness that we can approach him.

It seems that we are in the temple courts now. At this point, the song turns to the theme of waiting on God. 'Wait' (v. 5) seems a strange verb, in a way, but we need to think of it in terms of expectantly watching, rather than passively waiting. This is a profound spiritual discipline. God's mercy, the revelation of his purposes for us, is as certain as the dawn that the watchmen on the city walls wait for through the night hours. They have to stay awake and be alert or they will miss the glorious first light of dawn.

There is a prayer in the Roman Catholic Mass that always touches me when I hear it. During the Lord's Prayer, after the petition 'and deliver us from evil', the priest picks up the prayer, asking that we may be delivered from all evil and know peace, 'as we wait in joyful hope for the coming of our Saviour Jesus Christ'. 'Waiting in joyful hope' is really what it is all about.

DAVID WINTER

Calm and quiet

O Lord, my heart is not lifted up, my eyes are not raised too high; I do not occupy myself with things too great and too marvellous for me. But I have calmed and quieted my soul, like a weaned child with its mother; my soul is like the weaned child that is with me. O Israel, hope in the Lord from this time on and for evermore.

This is a beautiful psalm, full of humble adoration and a deep sense of serene faith, but it is not easy to see why it is among the Songs of Ascent. It does not sound like a song that pilgrims would sing, nor does it immediately seem to be connected with the temple and the worship of God. Not only that, but many scholars have assumed it was written by a woman. The references to the weaned child and the modesty with which the writer adopts the position of a woman in biblical times ('I do not occupy myself with things too great… for me', v. 1) certainly point to that possibility.

It is also, however, the kind of prayer that might be uttered by anyone standing for the first time in the awesome setting of the temple, which, for Jews then, was the holiest place on earth. Naturally, they would be humbled by the experience, but also excited and tense. In these circumstances, how do we achieve the serenity of the truly prayerful spirit?

The writer has the answer, in the form of an experience that is familiar to mothers. The child is eager for milk, possibly crying for it, but the moment it starts suckling from its mother's breast, it goes still and quiet, absorbed with taking in the comforting and life-giving drink. The psalmist makes that her own experience, standing in the temple court—being 'calmed and quieted' like the 'weaned child that is with me' (v. 2). So, there in the temple, the psalmist seeks a similar experience to the baby's—excited, hungry, longing for sustenance, then suddenly stilled when that need is met and the presence of God himself nourishes the soul.

'Like newborn infants, long for the pure, spiritual milk, so that by it you may grow into salvation' (1 Peter 2:2).

DAVID WINTER

A place for the Lord

Rise up, O Lord, and go to your resting-place, you and the ark of your might. Let your priests be clothed with righteousness, and let your faithful shout for joy. For your servant David's sake do not turn away the face of your anointed one... For the Lord has chosen Zion; he has desired it for his habitation: 'This is my resting-place for ever; here I will reside, for I have desired it. I will abundantly bless its provisions; I will satisfy its poor with bread. Its priests I will clothe with salvation, and its faithful will shout for joy.'

This, by some way the longest of the Songs of Ascent, seems to be a song of praise on the occasion of the arrival of the ark of the Lord in the temple, where it would 'rest' in the Holy of Holies. The ark was a large wooden box overlaid with gold, surmounted by two cherubim and carried on two golden poles. No human hand was permitted to touch the box itself. The Israelites had brought it with them from their wilderness pilgrimage, during which it was housed in a huge tent known as the tabernacle. The ark symbolised for them the presence of God among his people. Since then, the ark had been housed in a tent at Kireath-jearim (the 'Jaar' of verse 6). The bringing of the ark into Jerusalem and its solemn installation in the holy place is the theme of this joyful song.

Of course they all knew that God did not 'live' in the temple. At its dedication, Solomon reminded the worshippers, in his great prayer of consecration, that 'even heaven, and the highest heaven, cannot contain you, much less this house that I have built!' (1 Kings 8:27). Yet, for all of us, there are particular places where we are more aware of the presence of God, and for the Jewish people that place was, beyond doubt, the temple. The ark represented the covenant by which he promised to be their God and took them to be his people.

Wherever God's people meet is holy ground.

DAVID WINTER

Praise in the holy place

How very good and pleasant it is when kindred live together in unity! It is like the precious oil on the head, running down upon the beard, on the beard of Aaron, running down over the collar of his robes. It is like the dew of Hermon, which falls on the mountains of Zion. For there the Lord ordained his blessing, life for evermore... Come, bless the Lord, all you servants of the Lord, who stand by night in the house of the Lord! Lift up your hands to the holy place, and bless the Lord. May the Lord, maker of heaven and earth, bless you from Zion.

As the pilgrims enter the temple, their first reaction is one of joy at their unity. 'Kindred' (Psalm 133:1) encompasses much more than simply members of a family. Jerusalem drew Jews from all over the Middle East as pilgrims to this holy place. As they walk and sing, someone recites a poem about the unity they all feel, even though their backgrounds and the languages they speak may be different. Their unity is a blessing, like the anointing oil at the consecration of a high priest or the precious dew from the northern hills that refreshes the hot and dry south. The group can look around and sense this blessing. I feel it in my local church every time we share the peace or gather at the Lord's table. Truly, 'there the Lord ordained his blessing' (v. 3).

Then perhaps another member of the party has a song, this time remembering those who minister in the temple. There is a special thanksgiving for the night shift—the priests who offer their prayers to God to keep Israel through the silent hours of the night. The song encourages them to lift up their hands in prayer and praise. Finally, the whole group, it seems, joins in uttering a blessing from the holy place.

Look around you in church or your house or prayer group. Reflect on how much the people mean to you, and you to them, and be thankful.

DAVID WINTER

Songs of praise:
'Let all mortal flesh keep silence'

The hymn 'Let all mortal flesh keep silence' was originally an ancient chant of devotion to the Eucharist. The words of the hymn pointing principally to this theme are found in verse 2, but they are not the main thrust of the notes that follow. The hymn was inspired by words from Habakkuk 2:20: 'The Lord is in his holy temple; let all the earth keep silence before him!' The original was written in Greek, titled 'Prayer of the Cherubic Hymn', for the offertory in the Divine Liturgy of St James, which is very old, with a history going back to at least AD347.

Hymns Ancient and Modern: Revised recognises the hymn's original theme, placing it in a section devoted to Holy Communion, but the tune to which it is most commonly sung points to another association. Its title is 'Picardy', the melody of a traditional French carol. The musical arrangement that is most familiar to us today comes from the composer Ralph Vaughan Williams, set to words translated from the Greek by Gerald Moultrie, a Victorian public schoolmaster and Anglican hymnwriter. The Advent/Christmas theme of the hymn is particularly strong and I find it difficult to imagine a more perfect blend of words and music, with the plainchant bringing out powerfully the hymn's sense of awe-inspiring wonder.

It was the association with Advent/Christmas, rather than with Holy Communion, that first fired my imagination when I was a teenager. It was one of those hymns that, without at the time knowing why it should be, gave me goosebumps. It is only recently that I became more consciously aware of what my younger self instinctively sensed.

So much of our lives, both inside and outside church, has a tendency to become earthbound. We get so tied up in the practicalities and minutiae of everyday life that we forget to lift our eyes to the heavens. 'Let all mortal flesh keep silence' reminds us that the divine reality is at work, both in and beyond the most intimately familiar things—a reality that challenges us to listen and worship, allowing ourselves be held and nurtured in the healing and transforming silence of God.

BARBARA MOSSE

Let all mortal flesh keep silence,
and with fear and trembling stand;
ponder nothing earthly minded,
for with blessing in his hand,
Christ our God to earth descendeth
our full homage to demand.

King of kings, yet born of Mary,
as of old on earth he stood,
Lord of lords, in human vesture,
in the body and the blood;
he will give to all the faithful
his own self for heavenly food.

Rank on rank the host of heaven
spreads its vanguard on the way,
as the Light of light descendeth
from the realms of endless day,
that the powers of hell may vanish
as the darkness clears away.

At his feet the six-winged seraph,
cherubim with sleepless eye,
veil their faces to the presence,
as with ceaseless voice they cry:
Alleluia, Alleluia
Alleluia, Lord Most High!

A sound of sheer silence

[The Lord] said [to Elijah], 'Go out and stand on the mountain before the Lord, for the Lord is about to pass by.' Now there was a great wind, so strong that it was splitting mountains and breaking rocks in pieces before the Lord, but the Lord was not in the wind; and after the wind an earthquake, but the Lord was not in the earthquake; and after the earthquake a fire, but the Lord was not in the fire; and after the fire a sound of sheer silence.

'Let all mortal flesh keep silence…' These words in the first line of the hymn have a haunting beauty and the singing of them may remind us that Christmas will soon be upon us. How easy, though, do we find it to apply them to ourselves, with our busy and noisy lives? Faced with demands on our time both inside and outside church, a teaching that asks us to wait on God in silence may seem like an impossible ideal—even if we see it as desirable.

Scripture, if we will allow it to speak to us, directs us a different way. In today's passage, the prophet Elijah is depressed, discouraged and in flight from the vengeful Jezebel. Standing alone on the mountain, he encounters God—not in the wind, earthquake or fire, as perhaps he might have expected, but in 'a sound of sheer silence' (v. 12). It is in that silence, rather than in the pyrotechnics of the natural world, that Elijah's recovery begins.

When we pray alone to God or come together in prayer and worship, it seems that we often feel we must fill the silence with our own all-too-many words. What are we afraid of, I wonder? Perhaps it is because today's episode from the story of Elijah reminds us that, despite our best efforts, the presence and activity of God in our midst are not ours to control. The story challenges us, as Elijah was challenged, to take time to step aside from the clamour of our daily lives and be quiet so that we can truly listen to the God who lives within us, in 'a sound of sheer silence' (v. 12).

'For God alone my soul waits in silence; from him comes my salvation'
(Psalm 62:1).

BARBARA MOSSE

65

We stand on holy ground

Moses... led his flock beyond the wilderness, and came to Horeb, the mountain of God. There the angel of the Lord appeared to him in a flame of fire out of a bush; he looked, and the bush was blazing, yet it was not consumed... When the Lord saw that he had turned aside to see, God called to him out of the bush, 'Moses, Moses!' And he said, 'Here I am.' Then he said, 'Come no closer! Remove the sandals from your feet, for the place on which you are standing is holy ground. He said further, 'I am the God of your father, the God of Abraham, the God of Isaac, and the God of Jacob.' And Moses hid his face, for he was afraid to look at God.

'And with fear and trembling stand...' After the hymn's opening exhortation to us to keep silence, in the second line and today's passage we are urged to stand before the awesome presence of God with 'fear and trembling'. This phenomenon should not be confused with our normal human reaction to frightening or dangerous experiences. Rather, it is to do with what the scholar Walter Brueggemann has called 'the crushing, awesome reality of God's holiness'. To 'remove the sandals from your feet' (v. 5) before him serves as an act of both recognition and willing submission. We quickly realise that Moses' experience is no ordinary happening. A bush burns but is not burnt, and an angel appears in the burning bush, focusing Moses' attention before God himself speaks to him. Moses' response is simply, 'Here I am' (v. 4).

God met Moses as he was tending the sheep—the normal routine of his working day. Do we expect God to meet us in the familiar pattern of our days—at home, at work, at school or university? Our own 'burning bush' may well be visible only to the eyes of faith, but Moses' experience challenges us to look out for it and acknowledge the presence and glory of God that surround us in all we do.

'Therefore, since we are receiving a kingdom that cannot be shaken, let us give thanks, by which we offer to God an acceptable worship with reverence and awe, for indeed our God is a consuming fire'
(Hebrews 12:28).

BARBARA MOSSE

With Christ in God

So if you have been raised with Christ, seek the things that are above, where Christ is, seated at the right hand of God. Set your minds on things that are above, not on things that are on earth, for you have died, and your life is hidden with Christ in God. When Christ who is your life is revealed, then you also will be revealed with him in glory.

'Ponder nothing earthly minded…' Teachings such as these sometimes get a bad press because people assume that we are being told to have nothing to do with other people or the concrete experiences of our daily lives; we should instead spend all our time in prayer. Indeed, this view is that committed prayer (unless it takes the form of active intercession) is assumed to be incompatible with a life of practical service in society. Comments such as, 'She's too heavenly minded to be any earthly good' come to mind.

Such views suggest a misunderstanding of both the teaching in Colossians and the message of the third line of the hymn. Paul's urging to heavenly mindedness rather than earthly does not stem from hatred of the world, but is, instead, motivated by the priority of the Christian's relationship with Jesus, the Lord of the Church. It is when we focus on Christ and 'strive first for the kingdom of God' (Matthew 6:33) that the warp and weft of our lives and relationships with one another fall into place. As the letter moves on towards its conclusion, it becomes clear that 'heavenly mindedness' does not imply an abdication from our ordinary lives in society; far from it. It is instead our primary rootedness in Christ, who in God is the originator and controller of all human history, that the earth will be transformed and brought to its final and glorious consummation.

'As God's chosen ones, holy and beloved, clothe yourselves with compassion, kindness, humility, meekness, and patience. Bear with one another and… forgive each other; just as the Lord has forgiven you… Above all, clothe yourselves with love, which binds everything together in perfect harmony. And let the peace of Christ rule in your hearts… And be thankful' (Colossians 3:12–15, abridged).

BARBARA MOSSE

Light in the darkness

In the beginning was the Word, and the Word was with God, and the
Word was God. He was in the beginning with God... The true light,
which enlightens everyone, was coming into the world. He was in the
world, and the world came into being through him; yet the world did
not know him. He came to what was his own, and his own people did
not accept him. But to all who received him, who believed in his name,
he gave power to become children of God... And the Word became
flesh and lived among us... full of grace and truth.

'For with blessings in his hand, Christ our God to earth descendeth.'
Unlike the other three Gospels, the beginning of John's Gospel places
Christ in a cosmic context: 'In the beginning was the Word' (v. 1).
John's prologue traces the story as this Word is born on earth as Jesus
of Nazareth: 'And the Word became flesh and lived among us' (v. 14).

The fourth and fifth lines of the hymn name Christ, meaning 'the
anointed one', explicitly. What does the hymn mean when it states that
Christ comes 'with blessings in his hand'? Today's passage from John
offers a possible answer when it claims that those who received and
believed in Christ were given 'power to become children of God' (v. 12).

We may perhaps wonder why so many do not accept Christ's blessings or simply do not see them, but, as the contemporary American
scholar Cornelius Plantinga Jr points out, the Christ we see in the
Gospels is 'elusive, unpredictable, untameable, unguessable'. He teaches
enigmatically in parables and riddles and, at times, even his closest
disciples have to ask him to explain his meaning (Luke 8:9–15). Christ
is there for all, but he constantly defies our attempts to domesticate or
contain him. We are encouraged to actively seek him, and allow him to
lead us beyond the limits of our human understanding into the depths
of the mystery that is God.

---

*'The mystery that has been hidden throughout the ages... has now been
revealed to his saints. To them God chose to make known how great
among the Gentiles are the riches of the glory of this mystery, which is
Christ in you, the hope of glory' (Colossians 1:26–27, abridged).*

BARBARA MOSSE

Great love

A woman in the city, who was a sinner, having learned that [Jesus] was eating in the Pharisee's house, brought an alabaster jar of ointment. She... began to bathe his feet with her tears and to dry them with her hair. Then she continued kissing his feet and anointing them with the ointment... [The Pharisee] said to himself, 'If this man were a prophet, he would have known who and what kind of woman this is... that she is a sinner.'... Jesus said to him, '... Do you see this woman? I entered your house; you gave me no water for my feet, but she has bathed my feet with her tears and dried them with her hair... I tell you, her sins, which were many, have been forgiven; hence she has shown great love. But the one to whom little is forgiven, loves little.'

'Our full homage to demand.' We may have been carried away by the beauty of the hymn's poetic turn of phrase so far, but this last line of the first verse should bring us up short. Christ has not come to earth simply to convey blessings but also to demand our full worship, reverence and commitment. We may well balk at the word 'demand'. We are busy people with many demands already on our time and money; surely it is enough simply to give what we feel we can manage?

The hymn, together with today's passage from Luke, offers an uncomfortable challenge to this view. Luke tells us of a nameless woman who has led a far-from-blameless life and comes to Jesus in a manner that shocks and scandalises his host. From his position of supposed superiority, the Pharisee condemns her and, along with her, Jesus for receiving her attentions with such grace and gratitude. Simon had invited Jesus to dine with him, but his hospitality has been sadly lacking. Simon and the woman represent to us the extremes of 'homage': the Pharisee, niggardly and grudging in his welcome; the woman, demonstrating a generosity and lavishness of love that puts the self-righteous Simon to shame. Where do we stand on this spectrum?

'Give, and it will be given to you. A good measure, pressed down, shaken together, running over, will be put into your lap; for the measure you give will be the measure you get back' (Luke 6:38).

BARBARA MOSSE

There was with the angel

In that region there were shepherds living in the fields, keeping watch over their flock by night. Then an angel of the Lord stood before them, and the glory of the Lord shone around them, and they were terrified. But the angel said to them, 'Do not be afraid; for see—I am bringing you good news of great joy for all the people: to you is born this day in the city of David a Saviour, who is the Messiah, the Lord…' And suddenly there was with the angel a multitude of the heavenly host, praising God and saying, 'Glory to God in the highest heaven, and on earth peace among those whom he favours!'

'Rank on rank the host of heaven spreads its vanguard on the way, as the Light of light descendeth from the realms of endless day, that the powers of hell may vanish as the darkness clears away.' This third verse of the hymn resonates strongly with today's passage from Luke, about the angels visiting the shepherds and telling them the good news of Christ's birth. In this, the shepherds, keeping watch in the darkness of the Bethlehem night, are connected with the age-old experience of the Old Testament people, who waited in darkness before the dawning of a great light (Isaiah 9:2). In Luke, a solitary angel conveys the message, which is then reinforced by the praises of 'a multitude of the heavenly host' (2:13). The hymn echoes this in its phrase 'rank on rank' describing the host of heaven, heralding the descent of the 'Light of light', which 'clears away' the darkness.

'Angelophanies' are, of course, nothing new. From the mysterious visits to Abraham (Genesis 18:1–15) and Moses (Exodus 3:1–2) to the angelic annunciations in Luke 1, the words spoken provide a divine interpretation of the mysterious events being experienced by those they are visiting. In today's passage, the contrast between the humble setting of Christ's birth and the glory and grandeur of the angelic proclamation could hardly be greater.

'Since we are surrounded by so great a cloud of witnesses, let us also lay aside every weight and the sin that clings so closely, and let us run with perseverance the race that is set before us, looking to Jesus' (Hebrews 12:1).

BARBARA MOSSE

Hallelujah!

And the twenty-four elders and the four living creatures fell down and worshipped God who is seated on the throne, saying, 'Amen. Hallelujah!' And from the throne came a voice saying, 'Praise our God, all you his servants, and all who fear him, small and great.' Then I heard what seemed to be the voice of a great multitude, like the sound of many waters and like the sound of mighty thunder-peals, crying out, 'Hallelujah! For the Lord our God the Almighty reigns.'

'At his feet the six-winged seraph, cherubim with sleepless eye, veil their faces to the Presence, as with ceaseless voice they cry: Alleluia, Allelluia, Alleluia, Lord Most High!' This worship is the glorious end to which everything leads. This final verse of the hymn, reflecting John's Gospel, has taken us on quite a journey. It began by urging our silent awe and wonder at the mysterious descent of Christ from heaven to earth (v. 1). Crucial events in Christ's earthly life and their significance follow (v. 2, not explored here). Then, with the final two verses, we are swept back up to heaven, to the angels who herald Christ's coming (v. 3) and the final consummation, when God will be seen to reign supreme over all (v. 4). The final verse captures the praise and wonder this will excite, and the reference to the 'six-winged seraph' picks up the graphic picture-language of Isaiah's vision in the temple (Isaiah 6:1–3).

Revelation 19 looks forward into a glorious future beyond our imagination when all our sorrow and pain, worry and anxiety will be things of the past. 'Hallelujah!' (v. 4) will be the only response we can give as we are swept up into a full realisation of the love and eternal purposes of God. Then perhaps, once again, we may feel moved to silent adoration as, before the throne of God, we might cite the words of another well-loved hymn: 'lost in wonder, love and praise.'

'In the year that King Uzziah died, I saw the Lord sitting on a throne…
Seraphs were in attendance above him… And one called to another
and said: "Holy, holy, holy is the Lord of hosts; the whole earth is full
of his glory"' (Isaiah 6:1–3, abridged).

BARBARA MOSSE

Lost and found in Luke's Gospel

Human life is threaded with experiences of losing and finding, letting go and rediscovering, leaving things behind and moving on to new encounters, getting lost and being found. These experiences relate to a wide variety of things: relationships and people, material possessions, jobs, health, hopes and dreams. We may well, at various points in our lives, lose and recover our sense of purpose, understanding of ourselves and even perception of whether or not we are loved. Sometimes the losses will be difficult, painful and sad. Other times the letting go will release new energy and excitement about the future.

Many phases in our lives will be a mixture of all these things. What we make of it all will make us who we are. If we are people of faith, we will want to respond in a way that reflects our growing relationship with God. More than that, we will want to allow what happens to us to shape that relationship as we continually ask ourselves, 'Through all of this, what can I learn about God and what can God teach me about myself, others and the world?'

The Gospels are a rich source of reflection on our own life stories. As we immerse ourselves in Jesus' life and teaching, observing his interactions with a wide range of people, his understanding of the world and his relationship with the Father, we notice how his life story interweaves and resonates with our own. Luke's Gospel is a broad and deep treasury of resources on the theme of losing and finding, which recurs in Jesus' parables, teaching, healings and human encounters. Whether or not Luke was conscious of this, he offers us many ways to reflect on our own experiences of losing, being lost, finding and being found.

Most of all, perhaps, his Gospel reveals in Jesus a picture of the God who knows intimately the human experiences of loss and recovery and who longs for us to know that, however lost we sometimes feel, we are in fact sought out, recovered and fully known—for ever and unwaveringly found.

ROSEMARY LAIN-PRIESTLEY

Moving on

[Zechariah] asked for a writing-tablet and wrote, 'His name is John.' And all of them were amazed. Immediately his mouth was opened and his tongue freed, and he began to speak, praising God.

At the retirement party of a friend, I was struck by the fact that the focus was not simply on saying goodbye (though, of course, this was part of what happened), nor on growing old in the next phase of life, but, rather, 'growing new'.

Elizabeth and Zechariah were getting on in years when they were given a wholly new and unexpected challenge to face. A tremendously exciting and positive one, but probably coming as quite a shock! In order to receive their gift of parenthood they would certainly have had to 'grow new' as well as older. No longer could they choose a pace of life suited to age and diminished energy or make plans without taking account of anyone else, or even just sleep in when they felt like it.

Perhaps it is nervousness as well as wonder that makes Zechariah ask the angel, 'How will I know that this is so?' (v. 18). His doubts are quite literally silenced and he is embarrassed to find himself voiceless when he emerges to face his neighbours.

Months later, with the coming of the child, Zechariah remembers his conversation with God's messenger and names his son accordingly. During his imposed silence he has, no doubt, been on a journey, gathering the faith to believe that what has been promised is possible, perhaps doing an audit of what must be left behind as life moves forward. As he regains confidence in himself and God, he also finds his voice.

The greatest gifts and graces of our lives can come at odd, even inconvenient, times. Embracing them fully, trusting in the unknown tomorrows, is an act of courage as well as joy—a God-infused experience of letting go as well as finding.

Help me to live in the knowledge that your timing, though sometimes awkward for me, is right. Grant me strength to deal with loss, and courage to welcome the future and the opportunity to 'grow new'.

ROSEMARY LAIN-PRIESTLEY

Change of plan

Mary said to the angel, 'How can this be, since I am a virgin?' The angel said to her, 'The Holy Spirit will come upon you, and the power of the Most High will overshadow you; therefore the child to be born will be holy; he will be called Son of God.'

The idea that we are in control of our lives is mostly an illusion. Of course there are choices and decisions we can make that will set a particular course of events in motion, protect us to an extent from danger or open up new possibilities, but, when the chips are down, there is an awful lot that lies beyond our control.

At this very early stage in Mary's life, God makes her an offer: an unplanned pregnancy before marriage, so that she can be the vehicle for God's astonishing new intimacy with the world. Could she have played safe, politely declined the invitation and sent the angel elsewhere to look for another willing partner in God's risky venture? Possibly, but she decides differently—perhaps recognising that none of us is ultimately in control of very much—and chooses to embrace the unknown.

Mary has a heart supple for God, a heart that recognises God's presence. Bending gracefully to God's prompting, she chooses the riskier road. She seems to intuit that to be willingly and trustfully held in God's hand is preferable to deluding ourselves that we can drive our own destiny.

What gains there were for the whole of humanity as a result of Mary's brave response to God's finding of her, and her finding of her place in God's plan! The incarnation, God becoming interwoven with the stuff of the world, was made possible by her willingness to relinquish her teenage dreams for new ones.

Mary let go of one future and yielded to the possibilities of another. Through the miracle of her 'Yes', the world gained a new future, too.

We all dream dreams of our future. Sometimes they coincide with God's purposes, but sometimes our visions miss the mark and we have to let go of them. How might we nurture in ourselves a heart supple enough to respond to God's best plans?

ROSEMARY LAIN-PRIESTLEY

Waiting and finding

Simeon took him in his arms and praised God, saying, 'Master, now you are dismissing your servant in peace, according to your word.'

When Jesus' parents took him to the temple for the ritual of purification, there were two people present who knew the significance of that day. Simeon was a holy and insightful man who believed that God intended to reveal the Messiah to him before his death. He was elderly and must have wondered how much longer he was going to have to remain patient. The prophet Anna, from a long line of prophets, was 84 and always in the temple, fasting and praying. Their lives had been so wholly orientated towards God that both of them immediately recognised who Jesus was.

Sometimes the need to pray, wait and simply be in God's presence is squeezed out by the many important tasks and projects that can so easily fill our lives. We might even feel that time spent just thinking and reflecting is time lost or frittered away, but nothing that helps to orientate ourselves in God's direction can ever be a waste of time. The whole meaning of our lives is to be found in God's creative love, hence our inbuilt longing—shared by Anna and Simeon—to discover signs of God's presence all around us. This takes time and patience, a gradual attuning to God over a lifetime.

For these two attentive servants of God, that longing to know God's presence was met in the most amazing way: in the life of a tiny baby, right there with them, present in the temple with his family. We have Simeon's words as a record of what they both knew: they had found the one in whose hope Israel lay, their time of waiting was over and they could rejoice and be ready to let go of life peacefully, knowing God was among his people.

Sometimes we may need to slow down and make space in our lives if we are to glimpse the divine in the extraordinariness of the everyday. How might I turn aside from busyness in order to see past the surface of things to the presence of God within?

ROSEMARY LAIN-PRIESTLEY

At home with God

When his parents saw him they were astonished; and his mother said to him, 'Child, why have you treated us like this? Look, your father and I have been searching for you in great anxiety.' He said to them, 'Why were you searching for me? Did you not know that I must be in my Father's house?'

On their journey back to Nazareth after visiting Jerusalem for the festival of Passover, Jesus' parents discover that he is not among the crowd of travellers. Their fear of losing a child reaches across the centuries and chills our hearts, but we know the end of the story, even as we read the beginning, and their loss, though terrifying, is temporary.

When they eventually found him, Joseph and Mary must have wondered what on earth Jesus meant by referring to the temple as his 'Father's house' (v. 49)—surely that was in Nazareth, the family home. It was a place of safety and nurture for a growing adolescent boy and they were, no doubt, longing to take him back there after this unnerving escapade.

Jesus, however, is on to a truth that will stay with him in all the places to which his calling leads. The truth is that in God's company we are never lost and it is exactly there that we should expect to find one another. As he will later teach others, the touch of God's hand is to be found everywhere—in the birds of the air and the lilies of the field, among the poorest and most marginalised of people, in the company of thousands or on a small boat with friends in a storm. God is always present and we are therefore always at home.

Perhaps the episode in the temple teaches us that to enjoy God's company to the full, we might sometimes have to stay behind after the crowds have left, step aside, ignore the constraints of the schedule, hang around a little longer, resist being where everyone else wants to be. Perhaps it might be wise, though, to tell others of our plans!

In what places might you deliberately linger, to experience God's presence more fully? Decide when you are next going there.

ROSEMARY LAIN-PRIESTLEY

The wrong sort of power

Then the devil led him up and showed him in an instant all the
kingdoms of the world. And the devil said to him, 'To you I will give
their glory and all this authority... If you, then, will worship me, it will
all be yours.' Jesus answered him, 'It is written, "Worship the Lord your
God, and serve only him."'

Jesus, after his baptism, is led by the Spirit into the wilderness.
There, the devil offers him everything. Jesus can have the whole
world, all the wonder of it and all power over it, if he will worship
Satan. Jesus knows that gaining everything will mean losing everything, however, so he tells the devil that he can worship and serve
only God.

What would Jesus have lost if he had entered the devil's pact and
gained the world? He would have lost his relationship with God and
that, of course, is everything. To turn away from the one who, at his
baptism, called him a beloved Son would have been to turn away from
life and from the particular life to which he had been called. Anything
gained would have been a hollow and empty prize because what Jesus
came to show the world was that the whole created universe finds its
meaning and purpose in God. A world distracted by the devil can never
have coherence or meaning.

Jesus is beginning to know that this is what his life is for: to proclaim the good news of God's utter, non-negotiable, unassailable love.
So, in the midst of temptation, he hangs on to the sense of the truth of
his own being—that he is beloved by God—in order to find the
strength to turn down power and glory. The wrong sort of power and
the wrong sort of glory are ultimately an illusion that lead to loss, emptiness and confusion rather than the fullness of being found and knowing our purpose and the meaning of our lives.

---

*When I find myself within reach of influence and power, remind me
to ask myself where and from whom it comes. Help me to use what
influence I have as a blessing to others and point them towards
God's transforming love. Amen*

ROSEMARY LAIN-PRIESTLEY

Letting down the nets

When [Jesus] had finished speaking, he said to Simon, 'Put out into the deep water and let down your nets for a catch.'... When they had brought their boats to shore, they left everything and followed him.

Sitting in the fishing boat a little way out on the lake, as Jesus taught the people gathered on the shore, what was Simon thinking? Was he preoccupied by the memory of the failed night's fishing he had just experienced? Hour after precious hour passing by, with nothing to show for it but tiredness and frustration?

If he was snoozing or daydreaming, something certainly woke Simon up. Perhaps it was Jesus' compelling stories, his intimate knowledge of God interweaving himself with the detail of the world. More than that, there was the authority with which Jesus directed the fishermen to the riches below the surface of the lake—to a feast where, just a few hours before, there had been famine. Having hauled in the abundant catch, the men simply left it all behind and followed Jesus, apparently without the need either to capitalise on their windfall or to know where they were going. They had found abundance once; perhaps they knew they would find it again, so long as they stuck close with their new friend.

In times of emptiness and frustration, when our activities, however focused and however much effort we put in, are just not bearing fruit, it may require a particularly attentive sort of listening for us to recognise that God is speaking to us. We may need to stop, sit consciously with Jesus and absorb his presence, opening ourselves to receive an unexpected instruction or be prompted toward a change of direction.

The familiarity of a task, relationship or situation can be a barrier to seeing new possibilities. Shifting our focus to Jesus can shake us awake and be the key to discerning a way forward, together with summoning the courage to leave behind the things we no longer need, trusting in God's abundant provision for whatever might come next.

Give me patience to listen attentively and wholeheartedly, courage to leave the shallows for the unknown depths and wisdom to know what I should and should not leave behind. Amen

ROSEMARY LAIN-PRIESTLEY

A strange sort of blessing

Then he looked up at his disciples and said: 'Blessed are you who are poor, for yours is the kingdom of God. Blessed are you who are hungry now, for you will be filled. Blessed are you who weep now, for you will laugh.'

There is something completely countercultural about the passage we have come to call the Beatitudes, or 'the blesseds'. The poor and hungry, those who weep and those who are persecuted are blessed, says Jesus. The kingdom of God belongs to them.

What does this mean? If those are our circumstances, we are unlikely to feel blessed. Jesus was not in the habit of being insensitive to the realities of people's lives, so the Beatitudes must be more than an empty promise that 'if God loves you, you will be OK.' Somehow, they are intended to frame life differently.

I heard a woman, looking back on several decades of life, speak of some devastating times—in particular, two bereavements that could have permanently crushed all joy from her. She did not underplay one bit the depth of her losses. Yet, she said that she sensed Jesus walking with her through all of it—a belief strengthened by the faithful presence of friends who, somehow, mediated God's love.

At the beginning of his public ministry, Jesus told the worshippers in the synagogue at Nazareth that he was there to bring hope to the blind, the poor, captives and the oppressed. Throughout Luke's Gospel, we see Jesus consistently seeking out and finding these people and changing their lives by his healing presence.

People are not blessed by pain, but they may be blessed in their pain by the presence of others who walk with them, as well as God, who holds us all in an unfaltering grip. This is not a thought to be insensitively imposed by the 'obviously and outwardly blessed' on the destitute and suffering. Part of our discipleship is to walk alongside those for whom life is full of loss and, with them, find that God is there.

Who do we know who needs someone to walk alongside them through difficult times? How might we do this with sensitivity and love?

ROSEMARY LAIN-PRIESTLEY

Setting our compass by Jesus

'For those who want to save their life will lose it, and those who lose their life for my sake will save it. What does it profit them if they gain the whole world, but lose or forfeit themselves?'

Hard on the heels of Jesus' declaration that he is going to be killed and then raised from the dead come these difficult words to the disciples. Whether he means them literally or not, he is using the starkness of his own future to make it abundantly clear that no one can follow him half-heartedly. Far too much is at stake.

If we are serious about our relationship with Jesus, we should expect it to impact our lives at all levels. We will need to sit light to our preferred image of ourselves and be prepared to let go of habits and characteristics to which, through fear or inertia, we would much rather cling.

Luke follows this passage with the story of Jesus' transfiguration. The three disciples who are present see Jesus in dazzling white and Moses and Elijah 'in glory' (v. 31). There is a clarity to that vision, but then they are suddenly wrapped in a thick cloud, which is frightening and disorientating. From the cloud comes God's voice, proclaiming Jesus as his Son.

By listening to that voice, once the cloud lifts they should have a better understanding of who Jesus is and a tentative hope that, if he is knowingly heading into dangerous places, it is for God's purposes. Similarly, in order to know who we are and where we should be going, we need to orientate ourselves via Jesus. Only if we keep him firmly in our sights will we learn who he is and, therefore, who we are. But we need to be prepared for challenges, for time spent in the cloud and to lose as well as gain things on the way.

Teach me how to keep Jesus in my sights and give me the courage to follow him. Strengthen me to resist the diversions that so easily attract me. Help me to listen hard for the voice that will remind me who Jesus is and who I am, too. Amen

ROSEMARY LAIN-PRIESTLEY

The kindness of strangers

But a Samaritan while travelling came near him; and when he saw him, he was moved with pity. He went to him and bandaged his wounds, having poured oil and wine on them. Then he put him on his own animal, brought him to an inn, and took care of him.'

On All Saints' Day, some congregations remember those who are recognised as 'official' saints in the Christian story, some remember the saintly people they have known personally, and others do both. These different approaches reflect the fact that there are some saints who have been officially designated by the church and countless others who have walked or still do walk among us in everyday life.

If what makes a saint is a lifetime of seeking to grow into the likeness of Christ, then we are all called to sainthood. The parable of the good Samaritan is a lovely illustration of how we might rediscover the idea of sainthood as we let go of our assumptions about who might exercise it and what it might look like.

Imagine being in the direst of circumstances, like this traveller from Jerusalem to Jericho. Beaten up, stripped of everything, left for dead, alone—all he needs is one person whose heart is stirred by his plight.

He has no luck with the religious people, who give him a wide berth, but then a foreign national, from a region that has historic disputes with his own, finds him. Here the whole tone of the story changes. We know it so well that it no longer surprises us as it should.

One of the things that can raise our spirits on days when we are finding life difficult is the kindness of strangers. A chance encounter with a friendly person at the bus stop or the water cooler, or in the school playground, can turn our day around.

All human beings have the potential to express God's indiscriminate love. The kindness of strangers reminds us that saints walk unrecognised among us and we, too, are called to grow into God's likeness with courage and imagination.

Gracious God, teach me to receive from others, and offer to them, the simple, neighbourly goodness that sets us on the road to saintly living.

ROSEMARY LAIN-PRIESTLEY

Rich towards God

'But God said to him, "You fool! This very night your life is being demanded of you. And the things you have prepared, whose will they be?" So it is with those who store up treasures for themselves but are not rich towards God.'

A man asks Jesus to intervene in a dispute about inheritance. Instead of getting involved in family politics, Jesus points to the wider picture. He tells the story of a landowner whose crops are so abundant that he pulls down his own barns and builds bigger ones to store his excess harvest. What madness, Jesus points out, when the man could lose his life that night! He will have gained nothing from his riches.

At the beginning of the Judeo-Christian scriptures—just after creation—God gives people the task of stewarding the earth well and justly. So, we know that we should neither waste what we have nor hoard it. We are not always great at achieving this balance or recognising the times when we need to be cautious and those when we are being called to risky generosity.

None of us can decide on someone else's behalf what an appropriate amount of riches might be. 'Rich' is a relative concept: most of us are rich in comparison with the average refugee or our neighbour whose benefits have been cut. How do we even begin to calibrate the level of material comfort that is acceptable for a Christian?

We will all do it differently and there will be complex decisions to make about the perfectly appropriate enjoyment of life and our responsibility towards the rest of humanity. There will be times when, for the sake of those who depend on us, we give less away, but there will also be times when we know we must sit light to our blessings and live open-handedly, trusting that in loosening our grip we will rediscover God's generosity. If what we own begins to own us, then we lose everything that matters.

When I have more than I need, grant me a heart for giving.
When I am called to give sacrificially, help me to rise to that calling.
May I never allow what I own to begin to own me. Amen

ROSEMARY LAIN-PRIESTLEY

Bending the rules

But the Lord answered him and said, 'You hypocrites! Does not each of you on the sabbath untie his ox or his donkey from the manger, and lead it away to give it water? And ought not this woman, a daughter of Abraham whom Satan bound for eighteen long years, be set free from this bondage on the sabbath day?'

A woman has been crippled for 18 years, bent over, unable to stand up straight. She has lost the ability to scan the horizon, look around at the beauty and activity of the world or look into another person's eyes unless they are willing to contort themselves for her sake.

In healing this woman, Jesus restores to her the dignity of life and relationship that she has been missing for so long. He gives her back far more than her physical health. There is the possibility of renewed relationships and, quite literally, a new perspective on life. Yet, he is criticised by the leader of the synagogue—not for healing the woman, but doing so on the sabbath.

When Yahweh freed his people from hard labour in Egypt, the sabbath was one of his gifts to them—part of his covenant and a means of shaping their future for the better by encouraging a healthier way of living. The rhythm of six days of work followed by one of deep rest echoes the process of creation and marked the end of the drudgery inflicted by the pharaoh's regime. Sabbath signified freedom, the restoration of life and health, the recovery of a sense of perspective, and time for themselves and the enjoyment of their relationship with God.

Jesus' response to the synagogue rulers brings their peevishness into sharp relief. These people ensure the comfort of their animals on the sabbath, so what are they saying about this woman by insisting on treating her less well than their oxen? What riches have they lost from their own lives because of their ignorance of God's priorities and the narrowness of their vision?

Do you sometimes hide behind the rules because you are afraid of living life to the full? How might we use the gift of the sabbath to rediscover God's perspective on the world?

ROSEMARY LAIN-PRIESTLEY

God's tenacious love

'Which one of you, having a hundred sheep and losing one of them, does not leave the ninety-nine in the wilderness and go after the one that is lost until he finds it?... Or what woman having ten silver coins, if she loses one of them, does not light a lamp, sweep the house, and search carefully until she finds it?'

The parables of the lost sheep and lost coin leave us in no doubt about our infinite value to God. The shepherd appears to neglect the 99 while searching for the single woolly stray. The house is turned upside down for the coin, every corner swept and combed. The rejoicing is unlimited when the sheep and the coin—and the repentant sinner they represent—are finally found.

All sorts of things happen in life that can cause us to lose our sense of self-worth: broken relationships, tricky parenting experiences (as a parent or a child), a really difficult period at work or the knowledge, as the Confession in the Book of Common Prayer so beautifully puts it, that 'we have erred, and strayed from thy ways like lost sheep'. Whatever the cause, it can be very difficult to find the resources within ourselves to recover our equilibrium. We struggle with a profound sense of being lost, alone and unreachable.

It is in such times that we most need to recall those images of God as the distracted shepherd or distraught housewife, refusing to give up on us. God is unable to rest until the one who has lost their way, their mojo, their sense of self-in-relationship-with-God-and-others, has been rescued. Just sitting with such images in our mind can be the trigger for God's healing work to begin.

On the days when we hide beneath the surface of our lives, feeling fragile, there is still a thread that cannot be broken, connecting us to the God who never gives up on us and who longs for every child to know themselves found.

Revive in me the deeply felt knowledge of God as one who actively seeks me out when I hide. Renew in me the joy of being found. Restore in me the belief that I am loved. Amen

ROSEMARY LAIN-PRIESTLEY

A grace-filled way of living

'But we had to celebrate and rejoice, because this brother of yours was dead and has come to life; he was lost and has been found.'

Much ink and many pulpit hours have been spent on the parable of the prodigal son—or of the loving father, as it is sometimes renamed, or even 'the prodigal and his brother'.

We can call it what we like and place the emphasis as we prefer, because there are universal truths to be learned about the precarious adventure of growing up, the resentment that can rise unbidden in the heart of a 'loyal child', and the desolation we experience when we know we have wandered far from the people we love or the better self we know we could be.

All the characters in this story experience loss—of integrity, relationship, material security and the trust of other family members. When the prodigal returns, there is suddenly a reversal and a possible tipping point. All might be recovered, yet, equally, so much more might be lost if those involved are not able to dig deep and act with honesty and sensitivity towards one another. It would be understandable if the father chose to harden his heart rather than open himself to the possibility of more grief. The elder son might now estrange himself from the family if he refuses to forgive. The shame of the prodigal son might express itself in defensive bravado about his actions.

Most of us have moments in our lives when we face similar choices and the balance could tip either way. Awash with hurt, indignation or the need to save face, we can miss the moment when grace might break in. Loss can lead to more loss, just as God is poised to bring healing and recovery. In the parable, the father's words put it most clearly: 'This brother of yours was dead and has come to life; he was lost and has been found' (v. 32). May we never, because of resentment, stand in the way of God's healing.

In your own life, are there hurts or resentments that you need to let go? How might you encourage others in the recovery and healing of relationships?

ROSEMARY LAIN-PRIESTLEY

Welcoming Jesus in

When Jesus came to the place, he looked up and said to him, 'Zacchaeus, hurry and come down; for I must stay at your house today.' So he hurried down and was happy to welcome him.

Zacchaeus, like other tax collectors at that time, was rich because he bumped up the taxes to line his own pocket. It is unlikely that he had many friends and, on the day that Jesus visited Jericho, he found Zacchaeus alone—alone and up a tree because he was short and could not see over the crowds. The picture is of a solitary man, going about his work on his own, counting his money on his own, eating his meals on his own, watching the action from a special vantage point, but still on his own.

Yet, when Jesus calls him down from the tree, Zacchaeus seems ready, even eager, to respond to his request for hospitality. Perhaps the emptiness of his life has been gnawing away at him. Materially rich, he is, nevertheless, devoid of the connection, friendship and warmth that truly enriches human life.

Zacchaeus welcomes Jesus into his house. Then, prompted by his presence and apparently without being asked, he blurts out his intention to give half his possessions to the poor and pay back what he owes people four times over.

Jesus longs to enter our space, to receive our hospitality, to break bread with us, just as he did with Zacchaeus. But we have to be ready to respond; ready, too, to change as our relationship with him grows. Zacchaeus realises that he has become lost among his riches. His life has been impoverished by his focus on the wrong priorities. He can let them go now because he has been sought out and saved.

Welcoming Jesus into our hearts and homes can prompt unexpected changes in our lives. If we find the courage to let go of the things that used to define us, we will be freed to find new priorities and peace.

If we really let Jesus into our space—into our heart, our mind, our home—what are the areas of our life that we might find the confidence and motivation to work on and change?

ROSEMARY LAIN-PRIESTLEY

Revelation 1—4

The book of Revelation is a bit like Marmite: you either love it or you hate it. Some interpret it as a detailed prediction of what will happen in the 'end times' and usually think the time that they are living in qualifies. Some find it puzzling, extreme, best left alone. Both approaches limit its relevance.

Revelation is in the 'apocalypse' category of biblical literature, which appears now and then in the Old Testament, in parts of Ezekiel and Daniel, but really became popular in the period between the Old and New Testaments. The word does not mean 'end-of-the-world disaster', as it often does now (in the title of the film *Apocalypse Now*, for example), but simply 'unveiling' or, indeed, 'revelation'. Scholars generally think that its author, known as 'John the Divine', is unlikely to be the John of John's Gospel or even his letters. It was a common name then, as now. (My own son is called John!)

As with the Bible generally, Revelation applied first to those who first read or heard it. It was essentially a letter, like those by Paul, designed to challenge and encourage those who received it. It was addressed to a people facing great oppression and wondering if they had taken the wrong path or if God had deserted them. Its dramatic imagery (a bit like a graphic novel) stands, first of all, for the geopolitical situation of the time, with 'Babylon' standing for the Roman Empire. Its first four chapters are very much directed at individual churches that existed at the time.

This does not mean, of course, that it cannot speak to us now or has not spoken to every oppressed, yet hopeful, people throughout history. It speaks of how power relations change, how it is the poorest and most vulnerable who always suffer most as a result of the politics of empire, yet how God is in charge of all and will protect his people. The powerful will always be tempted to exploit and oppress, so Revelation is relevant to all times and all places.

I once composed a six-word summary of its contents: 'All empires oppress; all empires fall'. To this my husband wisely added three more: 'Jesus is Lord.'

VERONICA ZUNDEL

Words to be obeyed

The revelation of Jesus Christ, which God gave him to show his servants what must soon take place; he made it known by sending his angel to his servant John, who testified to the word of God and to the testimony of Jesus Christ, even to all that he saw. Blessed is the one who reads aloud the words of the prophecy, and blessed are those who hear and who keep what is written in it; for the time is near.

When I write a book, I expect to have my name on the front page. John, however, headlines his book by identifying Jesus as its originator. Yes, John wrote the words down, but only as a description of the visions he had been given. It is 'the testimony of Jesus Christ' (v. 2) before it is the testimony of John.

John identifies his record clearly as 'prophecy' (v. 3)—a word that is often misused. It is not exactly a prediction about the future, as if it were a kind of divine horoscope; it is more about revealing the likely consequences of the present. The prophets exposed the realities of their time and announced what would happen if the behaviour of the people did not change, as well as offering reassurance and hope to those who were faithful. John also offers blessing to those who share his words, as visions from God are not just for private entertainment but for the community of his people.

The last four words of today's passage are intriguing. For some 2000 years, Christians have tried to work out when Jesus will return and whether or not 'the end times' are here. We have always been wrong. The point is to live as if the time is always near.

What would it mean to 'keep what is written' (v. 3) in Revelation? It is not, after all, a series of commands. I hope its meaning will emerge as you read the notes in the coming days. For now, note that Revelation was not written to encourage speculation or even fear, but to call forth obedience to the way of Jesus.

'A prophet is a person who accurately predicts the present.'
Do you agree?

VERONICA ZUNDEL

Who, where, why?

I, John, your brother who share with you in Jesus the persecution and the kingdom and the patient endurance, was on the island called Patmos because of the word of God and the testimony of Jesus. I was in the spirit on the Lord's day, and I heard behind me a loud voice like a trumpet saying, 'Write in a book what you see and send it to the seven churches, to Ephesus, to Smyrna, to Pergamum, to Thyatira, to Sardis, to Philadelphia, and to Laodicea.'

Gordon Welchman was a highly significant leader of the team at Bletchley Park that, during World War II, cracked Germany's 'Enigma' code. He started by studying the greetings in German messages and so worked out who was sending them, and where from and to, calling this 'traffic analysis'.

Studying the Bible is similar. We need to see where and who the message comes from and to whom it is addressed. John is writing from exile, during a time of persecution of the church. This is his context. He is experiencing isolation from his fellow believers, and his message is for the members of specific churches who are facing persecution. There are still many places in the world today where Christians live under constant threat of violence or state restrictions.

Jesus reminds us often that the calling of a prophet is not comfortable: 'In the same way they persecuted the prophets who were before you' (Matthew 5:12); 'Jerusalem, the city that kills the prophets and stones those who are sent to it!' (Matthew 23:37). Few societies want to hear hard truths about themselves, so they stop their ears to unwelcome challenges and may even start smear campaigns against those whose messages they do not like.

John's obedience costs him dearly. Yet, in the midst of loneliness and privation, he is 'in the spirit on the Lord's day' (v. 10). There is nowhere life can send us where God is not present. When have you sensed God's presence or gained spiritual insight in difficult circumstances?

Pray for those you consider to be speaking prophetically in today's society.

VERONICA ZUNDEL

Glory and humanity

Then I turned to see whose voice it was that spoke to me, and on turning I saw seven golden lampstands, and in the midst of the lampstands I saw one like the Son of Man, clothed with a long robe and with a golden sash across his chest. His head and his hair were white as white wool, white as snow; his eyes were like a flame of fire, his feet were like burnished bronze, refined as in a furnace, and his voice was like the sound of many waters. In his right hand he held seven stars, and from his mouth came a sharp, two-edged sword, and his face was like the sun shining with full force.

In a modern church building I know, there is a stained-glass window that attempts to portray this vision. I like it because it gets us away from portrayals of Jesus as a member of a specific race or culture, whether that is white with blond hair and blue eyes (which he certainly was not) or as a member of any other group.

Of course, a stained-glass window, even with the sun shining through it, can only hint at the splendour this passage conveys to the imagination. It is a blazing vision, addressing our sight, hearing and even our sense of touch.

Yet, even in this picture of the glorified Jesus, brighter than the transfiguration (Mark 9:2–3), Jesus is called 'the Son of Man' (Revelation 1:13)—a title he borrowed from Daniel (Daniel 7:13–14) and used of himself. It emphasises not his status as God, but his connection with humanity. This is beyond what any human being could actually look like, yet it is recognisably human.

The vision is rich with symbolic language: white for purity, fire for that which penetrates and consumes, the 'many waters' (Revelation 1:15) suggesting the voice of God, the sword representing the word and Spirit of God, the sun standing for the light of God and the warmth that gives life to all. Yet, somehow at the same time, it tells how, in Jesus, God has a human face.

Where do you find glimpses of both the glory of God and the humanity of Jesus?

VERONICA ZUNDEL

What we have seen and heard

When I saw him, I fell at his feet as though dead. But he placed his right hand on me, saying, 'Do not be afraid; I am the first and the last, and the living one. I was dead, and see, I am alive for ever and ever; and I have the keys of Death and of Hades. Now write what you have seen, what is, and what is to take place after this. As for the mystery of the seven stars that you saw in my right hand, and the seven golden lampstands: the seven stars are the angels of the seven churches, and the seven lampstands are the seven churches.'

'Write what you know' is the advice often given to writers like me, and it can work brilliantly, as in the works of Jane Austen, although some have also written wonderfully about situations far outside their experience. Sometimes, however, what you know is so overwhelming that it casts you right down, in awe or shame. That is John's understandable reaction to his dazzling vision.

Jesus' response is touching—literally. There is something so familiar and moving about his gesture of comfort, as we would naturally lay our hands on a distressed person. His words, too—perhaps the most common phrase in scripture, and often on the earthly Jesus' lips—'Do not be afraid' (v. 17). It is a command, at least in my life, more honoured in the breach than the observance, but is followed by a reassurance that, however much circumstances suggest the opposite, God is in charge and no one need be lost if they trust the one who has died and risen on their behalf.

The hand laid on someone for reassurance is also a hand of commissioning: 'Write what you have seen, what is, and what is to take place' (v. 19). It is a good instruction not only for writers but for anyone who wants to communicate an experience of God: describe your past experience, present life and future hope.

Lord Jesus, help me not to be afraid. Amen

VERONICA ZUNDEL

Love grown cold

'To the angel of the church in Ephesus write: These are the words of him who holds the seven stars in his right hand, who walks among the seven golden lampstands: I know your works, your toil and your patient endurance. I know that you cannot tolerate evildoers; you have tested those who claim to be apostles but are not... But I have this against you, that you have abandoned the love you had at first. Remember then from what you have fallen; repent, and do the works you did at first.... Let anyone who has an ear listen to what the Spirit is saying to the churches. To everyone who conquers, I will give permission to eat from the tree of life that is in the paradise of God.'

Long ago, I attended a weekend conference led by the late scholar Walter Wink on the letters to the churches in Revelation. He encouraged us to write a letter to the 'angel' (or spirit) of our own church, and then to draw it. My drawing showed a man with a mortarboard hat, a huge head and small body, endless instructions issuing from his mouth—and it proved to be a factor in our decision to leave that particular church.

Each letter in Revelation is a mixture of encouragement and reproof. Each also contains a description of Jesus' role and a promise to those who 'conquer'—that is, who remain faithful to Christ. All include the repeated phrase, 'Let anyone who has an ear listen', reminiscent of the way Jesus ended his parables.

Ephesus was a centre of pagan worship, its temple of Diana one of the seven wonders of the world. Its Christian community, founded by Paul, is commended for its patience and desire for true teaching, but reprimanded for its loss of love. Does this mean falling away from its enthusiasm for God? I don't think so, for, after 'repent', we do not read 'worship as you did at first' but 'do the works you did at first' (v. 5). The lost love is surely the people's love for each other and their neighbours. The reward for faithfulness is a privilege not even Adam and Eve had.

Jesus says to us, 'I know your works' (v. 19).

VERONICA ZUNDEL

Poor but rich

'And to the angel of the church in Smyrna write: These are the words of the first and the last, who was dead and came to life: I know your affliction and your poverty, even though you are rich. I know the slander on the part of those who say that they are Jews and are not, but are a synagogue of Satan. Do not fear what you are about to suffer. Beware, the devil is about to throw some of you into prison so that you may be tested, and for ten days you will have affliction. Be faithful until death, and I will give you the crown of life. Let anyone who has an ear listen to what the Spirit is saying to the churches. Whoever conquers will not be harmed by the second death.'

In the revelations of the 14th-century visionary Julian of Norwich, she writes, 'He said not "Thou shalt not be tempested, thou shalt not be travailed, thou shalt not be dis-eased"; but he said, "Thou shalt not be overcome".' Perhaps she had this letter to Smyrna in mind.

This is one of only two out of the seven letters in which there is no reproof, only praise and a prediction of persecution. Again, Jesus says, as he said to John himself, 'Do not fear' (v. 10). I find the phrase just before this—'I know your affliction' (v. 9)—deeply moving. It is easy, when life piles one problem or loss on another, to think God no longer notices what we are going through, but Jesus says, 'I know'. People often say those words when, in fact, they do not know, because they have not been through it, but Jesus really does know—he went through the worst physical and mental suffering human beings can inflict. 'You have… put my tears in your bottle,' says Psalm 56:8.

The church in Smyrna was financially poor, but this letter calls it rich—in gifts, which it was going to need when it was tested.

'For you know the generous act of our Lord Jesus Christ, that though he was rich, yet for your sakes he became poor, so that by his poverty you might become rich' (2 Corinthians 8:9). What 'riches' have you gained from him?

VERONICA ZUNDEL

What is in a name?

'And to the angel of the church in Pergamum write: These are the words of him who has the sharp two-edged sword: I know where you are living, where Satan's throne is. Yet you are holding fast to my name, and you did not deny your faith in me even in the days of Antipas my witness, my faithful one, who was killed among you, where Satan lives. But I have a few things against you: you have some there who hold to the teaching of Balaam, who taught Balak to put a stumbling-block before the people of Israel, so that they would eat food sacrificed to idols and practise fornication. So you also have some who hold to the teaching of the Nicolaitans. Repent then... To everyone who conquers I will give some of the hidden manna, and I will give a white stone, and on the white stone is written a new name that no one knows except the one who receives it.'

When I met her at college, a friend was using her middle name, so that is how I knew her. Then after graduating, she suddenly changed back to her first name. It was very confusing! 'A rose by any other name would smell as sweet,' wrote Shakespeare, but, in Jewish tradition, your name is your identity, so if you change it (as Saul did, to Paul) it means that you have a new life.

Pergamum was a powerful city—militarily, economically and culturally—with a splendid temple to Zeus. No doubt its citizens boasted of coming from there, but the Christians put their faith not in their location but in the name of Jesus, even when it might lead to death. Yet, there were those among them whose loyalty was compromised. It is interesting that the things this letter criticises in them are the very things forbidden in the letter to the Gentiles from the church council at Jerusalem (Acts 15:28–29).

We can find our core identity in family, status, education, career—or God.

Dear Father, you know my deepest identity. Help me to become a person worthy of the new name you will give me. Amen

VERONICA ZUNDEL

An all-seeing eye

'And to the angel of the church in Thyatira write: These are the words of the Son of God, who has eyes like a flame of fire, and whose feet are like burnished bronze: I know your works—your love, faith, service, and patient endurance. I know that your last works are greater than the first. But I have this against you: you tolerate that woman Jezebel, who… is teaching and beguiling my servants to practise fornication and to eat food sacrificed to idols. I gave her time to repent, but she refuses to repent of her fornication. Beware, I am throwing her on a bed, and those who commit adultery with her I am throwing into great distress, unless they repent of her doings; and I will strike her children dead. And all the churches will know that I am the one who searches minds and hearts, and I will give to each of you as your works deserve.'

Governments often talk of 'winning hearts and minds'—changing how people think and feel. Jesus talks here of searching minds and hearts. The description of his eyes and feet reinforces the idea that he can see all and go anywhere.

The church in Thyatira was loving and faithful, but there was a pagan influence. 'Jezebel' may have been an actual woman, but Thyatira, we know, was a city of trade and manufacturing, working with wool, linen, leather and bronze, making armour, dyeing, tanning, producing pottery and baking. The powerful trade guilds had a civic and religious role and 'worshipped' through sexual orgies. So, perhaps 'Jezebel' is a symbol of the people compromising by taking part in these practices.

We are ready to rebuke sexual sin in the church, but what about the other two great temptations—money and power? Do we think about the ethics of our jobs, our employers' policies, how we wield power in church, work and our families? 'Jezebel' has many faces and they are not all sexual.

The promise here 'to everyone who conquers' is that they will have 'authority over the nations' (v. 26), but first they have to be capable of being trusted to use that authority well.

In your mind, is the idea that God sees all a threat or a blessing?

VERONICA ZUNDEL

No deep secrets

'But to the rest of you in Thyatira, who do not hold this teaching, who have not learned what some call "the deep things of Satan", to you I say, I do not lay on you any other burden; only hold fast to what you have until I come. To everyone who conquers and continues to do my works to the end, I will give authority over the nations; to rule them with an iron rod, as when clay pots are shattered—even as I also received authority from my Father. To the one who conquers I will also give the morning star. Let anyone who has an ear listen to what the Spirit is saying to the churches.'

I remember my discomfort when a fellow student told me that he was rather attracted by the idea of 'esoteric knowledge', open only to a few. He is a Church of England priest now, so I hope he has changed his tune. He also thought he had been called to be celibate, but has been married for decades and has grown-up children.

To me, the idea that only a select few can have the 'inside knowledge' of our faith is contrary to everything Jesus stood for. Yes, in Mark's Gospel Jesus often tells the people he heals not to make it public, but that was for his own safety and so that he could continue his ministry, not because he wanted the good news to be restricted. Indeed, he constantly invites those excluded from the Jewish religion at the time to join his new community.

Of course, being in the 'in crowd' (while others are defined as 'out') is as seductive now as it was to the church in Thyatira, but it is not a Christian value. I have heard many references to 'the exclusive claims of Christ', but the other side of that is 'the inclusive call of Christ'. All are invited to the feast. Yes, Paul also talked about 'the mystery that was kept secret' (Romans 16:25), but he speaks of it as something now open to all.

'Hold fast to what you have' (Revelation 2:25). What are the things of faith that you need to hold on to?

VERONICA ZUNDEL

The living dead

'And to the angel of the church in Sardis write… I know your works; you have a name for being alive, but you are dead. Wake up, and strengthen what remains… for I have not found your works perfect in the sight of my God. Remember then what you received and heard; obey it, and repent. If you do not wake up, I will come like a thief, and you will not know at what hour I will come to you. Yet you have still a few persons in Sardis who have not soiled their clothes; they will walk with me, dressed in white, for they are worthy. If you conquer, you will be clothed like them in white robes, and I will not blot your name out of the book of life.'

My church might look to some like a dying church. Some 20 years ago, we regularly had 30 attenders; now we have twelve on a good Sunday. We still have great commitment to God and each other, however. We want to worship and serve God and draw others into our fellowship. Is that death?

I do not think this letter to Sardis is about numbers, but spiritual death. After all, Sardis has 'a name for being alive' (v. 1): it is a popular church. Yet, its members are failing to 'obey' what they have 'received and heard' (v. 3). It is their works (or lack of them), not their beliefs, that the letter questions. The gospel is not a set of things to believe; it is a person to follow, and, if we follow him, we should be doing as he did—bringing good news to the poor, caring for the sick, feeding the hungry, welcoming the homeless (Matthew 25:31–36).

Jesus will not judge our churches by how many people attend them, but by how much their life and ministry looks like his. Even as he castigates the Sardis Christians, he has praise and promises for a few. To 'soil our clothes' is to be 'clothed' with something other than the love, compassion and gentleness of Christ (Colossians 3:12–15).

Jesus, thank you that my name is in the book of life.
Help me to live up to it. Amen

VERONICA ZUNDEL

Open and shut

'And to the angel of the church in Philadelphia write: These are the words of the holy one, the true one, who has the key of David, who opens and no one will shut, who shuts and no one opens: I know your works. Look, I have set before you an open door, which no one is able to shut. I know that you have but little power, and yet you have kept my word and have not denied my name... Because you have kept my word of patient endurance, I will keep you from the hour of trial that is coming on the whole world to test the inhabitants of the earth... If you conquer, I will make you a pillar in the temple of my God; you will never go out of it.'

Soon we will be singing that beautiful ancient Advent hymn, 'O come, O come, Emmanuel', including the verse, 'O come, thou Key of David, come and open wide our heavenly home; make safe the way that leads on high and close the path to misery'. This is a great promise for those of us who have lived through a fair bit of misery.

The saying, 'When one door closes, another opens' has been parodied as, 'When one door closes, another shuts'! There are plenty of times in life when every door seems to be barred to us, yet here Jesus promises that what he opens, no one can shut, and what he closes, no one can open.

The church in Philadelphia, like that in Smyrna, is small and powerless, but the people are faithful, and God rewards faithfulness. 'There may be trouble ahead', as the song goes, but they will be protected. Our world is full of uncertainty—political, economic, environmental—but God promises certain redemption.

A pillar is a supporting structure, which is why Samson pushed down the pillars to demolish the Philistine temple. There are many apparently powerless groups of people who, by their prayers and faithful action, are God's 'pillars' of the new temple of God. We should not despise 'the day of small things' (Zechariah 4:10).

Which door would you like opened in your life and which one shut?

VERONICA ZUNDEL

Neither one thing nor the other

'And to the angel of the church in Laodicea write: The words of the Amen, the faithful and true witness, the origin of God's creation: I know your works; you are neither cold nor hot. I wish that you were either cold or hot. So, because you are lukewarm, and neither cold nor hot, I am about to spit you out of my mouth. For you say, 'I am rich, I have prospered, and I need nothing.' You do not realise that you are wretched, pitiable, poor, blind, and naked... I reprove and discipline those whom I love. Be earnest, therefore, and repent. Listen! I am standing at the door, knocking; if you hear my voice and open the door, I will come in to you and eat with you, and you with me. To the one who conquers I will give a place with me on my throne, just as I myself conquered and sat down with my Father on his throne.'

A famous painting by Holman Hunt, *The Light of the World*, shows Jesus with a lantern in his hand, knocking at an overgrown door. Significantly, there is no handle on the outside of the door: it can only be opened from inside.

The letter to the church at Laodicea makes several references to the city's features. Its natural waters were piped into a water system, but were tepid and unpleasant to drink; it was a banking centre, which explains the words 'I am rich'; it produced textiles, but Jesus calls the church 'naked'; it sold a salve for eye disorders, but Jesus calls them 'blind' (v. 17). This is the one letter in which he has nothing good to say about the church concerned. The people need to be 'reconverted', opening the door to Jesus.

This passage is sometimes used by Christians to label other Christians as 'wishy-washy' in their beliefs, but Jesus says, 'I know your works' (v. 15). He is disappointed with the way they live, rather than any heresy. This reminds me of Matthew 18:15–17, where, essentially, Jesus says, 'If someone is not living like a Christian, regard them as a non-Christian.' That implies not 'shun them', but 'witness to them'.

Lord, warm my love for you and my neighbour. Amen

VERONICA ZUNDEL

A glimpse of glory

After this I looked, and there in heaven a door stood open! And the first voice, which I had heard speaking to me like a trumpet, said, 'Come up here, and I will show you what must take place after this.' At once I was in the spirit, and there in heaven stood a throne, with one seated on the throne! And the one seated there looks like jasper and carnelian, and around the throne is a rainbow that looks like an emerald. Around the throne are twenty-four thrones, and seated on the thrones are twenty-four elders, dressed in white robes, with golden crowns on their heads. Coming from the throne are flashes of lightning, and rumblings and peals of thunder, and in front of the throne burn seven flaming torches, which are the seven spirits of God; and in front of the throne there is something like a sea of glass, like crystal.

When you were a child, did you imagine God as an old white-bearded man sitting on a throne? I did, but I did not believe in him! As I grew up and life threw me difficult events, my image of God developed and I began to believe. Nevertheless, we never really grow out of picture language: it generally makes things easier to imagine.

John sees a vision of the most precious and dazzling things he can think of, because God speaks to us in ways we can understand. Precious stones, a kingly throne, jewelled rainbow, white robes, gold crowns, sea of purest crystal glass—all these convey a glory beyond human imagination.

The 24 elders may stand for the twelve tribes of Israel and the twelve apostles or the 24 orders of priests or Levites. Either way, they represent all God's people and are given heavenly authority—an authority that does not dominate but serves. Coupled with thunder and lightning, it is a powerful yet alluring picture.

Perhaps this prepares us for the rest of the imagery of Revelation, which is about to become a lot stranger.

Whatever images we use of God, the reality is always bigger.

VERONICA ZUNDEL

Spiritual worship

Around the throne, and on each side of the throne, are four living creatures, full of eyes in front and behind: the first living creature like a lion, the second living creature like an ox, the third living creature with a face like a human face, and the fourth living creature like a flying eagle. And the four living creatures, each of them with six wings, are full of eyes all around and inside. Day and night without ceasing they sing, 'Holy, holy, holy, the Lord God the Almighty, who was and is and is to come.'... The twenty-four elders fall before the one who is seated on the throne and worship the one who lives forever and ever; they cast their crowns before the throne, singing, 'You are worthy, our Lord and God, to receive glory and honour and power, for you created all things, and by your will they existed and were created.'

In Graham Sutherland's great tapestry for Coventry Cathedral, these four creatures are memorably portrayed. The Jews thought they represented the orders of creation; Christians traditionally link them to the four evangelists, with Matthew being the man, Mark the lion, Luke the ox and John the eagle.

What might they mean to us? We could see their eyes as God's ability to be all-seeing, while their wings represent God's omnipresence. We could also see them as representing the angels or creation, giving ceaseless worship to God. The elders, who symbolise humanity, join their worship, surrendering their own glory by throwing down their crowns before God.

We do not yet see all humanity or all created things submitting to God (Romans 8:18–25), but, in John's vision, we see a foretaste of how all things will finally be brought under God's authority—not for punishment, but transformation (Colossians 1:15–20). Note how worship here is rooted in God's role as the Creator. In our churches, we often praise Jesus as our Redeemer, but how often do we praise God as the Creator?

I present my body as a living sacrifice, which is my spiritual worship (adapted from Romans 12:1).

VERONICA ZUNDEL

Job

The season of Advent focuses on the coming of God, but the word itself means more than 'coming'. *Venio* means 'come'. *Ad-venio* means 'to come against'. In these next two weeks, we will follow the ancient story of someone whose life and faith were suddenly up against it.

The ancient book of Job is an extended reflection on the vexed question of why bad things happen to good people. It is a story that challenges approaches to life and faith that are based on simplistic religious equations: do good and you will be blessed; do wrong and you will be cursed. The very fact that a traumatically painful personal story of undeserved tragedy is at the centre of this poem means we can never hide behind abstract theories or debate human suffering at a safe distance.

In the daily extracts from this long poem, we will meet a variety of characters and listen to varied attempts to explain what is happening and why. We will trace the challenges to faith when life is hard, and puzzle with Job over God's presence and purposes in the midst of human suffering.

Old Testament theologian John Goldingay journeyed with his first wife, Ann, for many years as she lived with, suffered and eventually died from multiple sclerosis. In his commentary on Job (*Job for Everyone*), he observes, from long experience, how 'in practice the answers that people tend to give people who are suffering usually fail to satisfy the sufferer in the way they satisfy the comforter. Much of the time what we need is the capacity to live with questions.' Job would agree. Perhaps you would, too.

In a sense, Job's story is everyone's in a world like ours. He brings us close to our own stories and those known to us. For this reason, following the story of Job takes courage. We need to be gentle with the places where it finds us. The challenge as we read it will be to hold the questions patiently, on an open hand, and not press too anxiously for 'answers'. After all, it was not answers that satisfied Job in the end.

DAVID RUNCORN

Meet Job

There was once a man... whose name was Job. [He] was blameless and upright, one who feared God and turned away from evil. There were born to him seven sons and three daughters. He had seven thousand sheep, three thousand camels... and very many servants; so that this man was the greatest of all the people of the east. His sons used to go and hold feasts... And when the feast days had run their course, Job would... rise early in the morning and offer burnt-offerings [for] them all; for Job said, 'It may be that my children have sinned, and cursed God in their hearts.' This is what Job always did.

The story begins on earth with a man called Job. Where and when this might have happened are not necessary details. It could be any time or place. What is important is the kind of person Job is. To be upright and blameless, to fear God and reject evil is a biblical summary of what faithful living requires of us. That Job's life is so abundantly blessed confirms this as the way of true blessing before God. To fear God in this sense is not to cringe, but is a deep reverencing— a life shaped around its true priorities.

Job's spiritual discipline is nothing if not thorough. Here is a man who, daily, offers sacrifices for the rest of his own family, just in case they sinned the night before. This could sound like rather controlling behaviour, but the whole description of his amazingly successful life is rather over the top, is it not? Perhaps it is meant to be, for what the storyteller is doing is carefully setting the scene for the story that follows. The point is made in unmistakable terms. Whatever is about to happen to Job, it cannot be anything to do with him deserving punishment or payback for something he has done wrong, or any loss or denial of faith on his part. This is a man of unblemished integrity and virtue. That kind of life should be blessed and secure, should it not?

I thank you, Lord, for those I know whose lives are a challenge to faith and a sign of your blessing. Amen

DAVID RUNCORN

A wager in heaven

One day the heavenly beings came to present themselves before the Lord, and Satan also came among them... The Lord said to Satan, 'Have you considered my servant Job? There is no one like him on the earth, a blameless and upright man who fears God and turns away from evil.' Then Satan answered... 'Does Job fear God for nothing? Have you not put a fence around him... and all that he has, on every side?... His possessions have increased in the land. But stretch out your hand now, and touch all that he has, and he will curse you to your face.' The Lord said to Satan, 'Very well, all that he has is in your power; only do not stretch out your hand against him!'

The scene has switched from earth to heaven. Out of sight and knowledge of Job—but not of us—the cosmic court is in session. Satan here is not to be confused with the figure of evil and rebellion against God that we meet in the New Testament. Here, he is a full member of God's heavenly council. His name means 'Accuser' and he functions as a sort of prosecuting counsel for God, under God's authority, probing and testing faith wherever he finds it. God boasts about Job's faithfulness. Job's godly credentials are repeated. 'Of course he is faithful,' says Satan. 'You treat him so well!' Surely Job is motivated by self-interest? Does Job really serve God without thought of personal gain?

Satan has a point. When we are finding the service we do for God rewarding, our prayers are being answered and we feel blessed, it is easy to be faithful. It is in the times when we feel let down or abandoned by God that our motives are tested.

Do we love for no reason? Real love does not seek reward. Real love is not in it for what it can get out. It has been said that there is a three-fold journey in our love of God. We begin by loving God for our own sake. We then learn to love ourselves for God's sake, but we must learn to love God for God's sake.

Lord, may I come to love you for your sake. Amen

DAVID RUNCORN

Meet Job's wife

Satan went out from the presence of the Lord, and inflicted loathsome sores on Job from the sole of his foot to the crown of his head. Job took a potsherd with which to scrape himself, and sat among the ashes. Then his wife said to him, 'Do you still persist in your integrity? Curse God, and die.' But he said to her, 'You speak as any foolish woman would speak. Shall we receive the good at the hand of God, and not receive the bad?' In all this Job did not sin with his lips.

This is the only place where Job's wife is heard. The one who loves and knows him best is left unnamed and not included among Job's comforters. She must be suffering, too. Do any friends gather around her?

To be the carer in a place of suffering is costly in its own way and can cause divisions in even the closest of relationships. We all respond to pain differently. Perhaps she speaks for those who must live with the consequences of other people's stories, choices and misfortunes. She challenges her husband's stubborn faithfulness, pointing out that if this is how God rewards faithful obedience, better to die! It is simply unendurable. Something to note here is that her response is directed at God and what God is doing. It is in contrast to the approach of Job's comforters.

Biblical faith is comfortable with anger and knows it may be the most honest place to begin. Many psalms start there (see Psalms 10 and 13), but Job dismisses his wife contemptuously. She is arguing like an empty-headed woman, he says. Her opinion is worthless. In his world, the serious matters of God and faith can be understood by men alone. She returns to silence.

Are there situations in which you can only watch, but you too suffer from what is happening? Can you relate to Job's wife and her response? Is there a difference between her anger and the sin that Job continues to resist? Perhaps he found the grace to apologise to her before the end.

Lord, I pray for what I am watching and sharing in the lives of those I love at the moment. Amen

DAVID RUNCORN

Meet Job's comforters

Now when Job's three friends heard of all these troubles that had come upon him, each set out from his home—Eliphaz the Temanite, Bildad the Shuhite, and Zophar the Naamathite. They met together to go and console and comfort him. When they saw him from a distance, they did not recognise him, and they raised their voices and wept aloud; they tore their robes and threw dust in the air upon their heads. They sat with him on the ground for seven days and seven nights, and no one spoke a word to him, for they saw that his suffering was very great.

Although it does not last, the first response of Job's friends is possibly their most appropriate. They arrive together, seeking to be a source of comfort to him. What they find totally overwhelms them. So grotesquely ravaged is Job that they actually do not know him at first. Anyone who has visited someone with a disfiguring injury or in intensive care knows the shock of just not recognising a once-familiar face. In expressions of grief that are less familiar to modern, Western societies, they respond with loud and dramatic distress, but then they just sit there with him—for seven whole days, silently.

The first task in the place of human pain is just to be there. That is harder than it sounds. It requires the willingness to be helpless and beyond words. We must resist the need to have the 'answers'. 'Weep with those who weep,' wrote Paul (Romans 12:15). He did not tell us to cheer them up. While our responses are driven by our anxiety to solve the problem (and so not to have to face it any more), we will not be truly present or listening. Our own anxious needs will be at the centre. Jesus pronounces a special blessing on those who mourn (Matthew 5:4). A capacity for grief is found at the heart of life in the kingdom.

Have there been times when you have been left speechless by the impact of terrible suffering? Can you think of times when others have simply been there with you in your own pain?

Lord, help me just to be present to what is happening,
without words or explanations. Amen

DAVID RUNCORN

Job despairs

[Job] cursed the day of his birth... 'Let the day perish on which I was born... Let that day be darkness!... Why did I not die at birth?... Why is light given to one in misery, and life to the bitter in soul, who long for death, but it does not come... Why is light given to one who cannot see the way, whom God has fenced in?... Truly the thing that I fear comes upon me, and what I dread befalls me... I am not at ease, nor am I quiet; I have no rest; but trouble comes.'

Having so recently dismissed his wife's urging to blame God for his terrible saga of tragedy and pain, Job's restraint finally gives way. He launches into a prolonged, angry rant at all that has happened to him. The depth of his bitterness and despair is truly shocking. He curses everything associated with his birth and calls on utter darkness to engulf every memory of his entry into the world. He rails at almost everyone and anything—his parents, the day, the night, the stars—everything that conspired to bring him into the life that he now finds unbearable. Why could he not have died at birth instead of coming to this?

At the beginning of the story, Satan accused God of fencing Job in with a blessed life (1:10). The word appears again here (3:23). Now, however, Job is fenced in by God in the sense of being trapped in a living hell, in which even the comfort of death is refused him. In all this he does not curse God. Interestingly, he hardly addresses God at all in this speech. But is that not where his complaint needs to be directed? In fact, he has not prayed at all since his suffering started, yet, 'Personal cries of pain and brash accusations against God are not thoughts to be hidden from the throne of God, but to be deposited with all their jagged edges and sharp cries before the face of God' (Beth LaNeel Tanner, in *Psalms and Practice*). In the end, it is the only safe place for them.

Can you think of a painful situation you are facing
and just tell God honestly how it feels?

DAVID RUNCORN

No easy answers

[Eliphaz said] 'Think now, who that was innocent ever perished? Or where were the upright cut off? As I have seen, those who plough iniquity and sow trouble reap the same. By the breath of God they perish, and by the blast of his anger they are consumed... There was silence, then I heard a voice: "Can mortals be righteous before God?"'

'What have I/they done to deserve this?' is a familiar question in the face of suffering. For Eliphaz, the first of Job's friends, there must be a reason. No one can claim to be 'right' before God, however. God acts as he wills.

Eliphaz has seen wanton living and says it always comes to a bad end. There is truth in what he says, and it is good news that our actions have consequences for which we are responsible. It means that life is not random. If it were, then everything that happened would be unconnected to any choices we make, good or bad. Life would be meaningless. Eliphaz's theology is inadequate, however, because we know that Job's suffering is happening to an innocent and exceptionally upright person. His story is outside any 'reward or punishment' understanding of how God acts.

Eliphaz's theology narrows further, the longer he argues. Towards the end, he is speaking of Job's suffering as God's correction and discipline (v. 17), but for what? He claims that the outcome will be blessing and healing, but what does that offer someone whose present suffering is all but destroying them? We must be wary of reaching for answers too quickly. We may end up being very clumsy with another's pain.

How would you respond to Eliphaz? God is God, but are his ways in our lives really governed by the inflexible pitiless logic of reward or punishment? They are certainly beyond our understanding and there are times when he allows us to go through painful experiences. Instead of trying to find reasons for what is happening, though, sometimes the only choice we have is to stop asking questions and exercise patience.

Lord, when there are no easy answers, help me to wait patiently
before you. Amen

DAVID RUNCORN

Asking the right question

Job again took up his discourse and said: 'O that I were as in the months of old, as in the days when God watched over me; when his lamp shone over my head, and by his light I walked through darkness; when I was in my prime, when the friendship of God was upon my tent; when the Almighty was still with me, when my children were around me; when my steps were washed with milk, and the rock poured out for me streams of oil!'

I remember a talk given by a pioneering hospice care doctor. In the discussion that followed, she simply sidestepped the predictable question about suffering and God, declaring that she had given up asking 'Why?' as it had never got her very far and she knew when she was beaten. Her task, she said, was just to immerse herself in what was actually happening. How would you have responded to receiving such an answer?

'Why?' and 'How?' are very natural questions when life hits us hard. 'How could this have happened?' 'Why me?' They are demands for an explanation of some sort, but do they actually help? The fiancé of a victim of a terrorist bombing on the London underground could not understand why she was on that train at all. It was not 'her train'. He kept asking, 'Why?' Then an underground employee remembered there was a points failure on her train line that morning. 'So she died because of a points failure', her fiancé said and wandered away in despair. 'The facts' simply deepened the anguish he felt and futility of her death.

It may not be answers we need. In the midst of life's rawest dilemmas, the challenge is to find ways to live more faithfully and deeply with the questions. So, it may be more helpful to ask, 'Where?' or 'In what ways?'—'Where may I find God or meaning in this?', 'In what ways am I to respond to what is happening to me?' These questions keep company with us on the journey in a way that explanations do not.

Lord, where are you in what is happening?

DAVID RUNCORN

Zophar speaks

Then Zophar the Naamathite answered: 'Should a multitude of words go unanswered?... Should your babble put others to silence, and when you mock, shall no one shame you? For you say, "My conduct is pure, and I am clean in God's sight." But O that God would speak, and open his lips to you, and that he would tell you the secrets of wisdom! For wisdom is many-sided. Know then that God exacts of you less than your guilt deserves.'

Eliphas could be called charismatic: he claims direct inspiration for what he says (4:12). Zophar, by contrast, is more likely to say, 'This is what the Church teaches', as if that settles the matter. If the teaching says that God blesses people who do right and punishes those who do wrong, then Job must have done something wrong or God would be blessing him. Job's experience appears to contradict that teaching, but Eliphas would reply that Job's understanding needs to change, not the teaching. There is an appealing simplicity to this logic.

We are already aware, however, that Job was written to expose how the traditional, authoritative answers do not always do justice to what is happening in real life. (They are useful starting places, though—we are not the first people to wrestle with such questions.) In Job, the traditional teaching, offered in the comments of his friends, constantly squeezes his life-events into explanations that plainly do not fit. There are parallels with the official teaching of Jesus' day. It resulted in love-less religion that imposed heavy demands on people's lives and offered no support in the process. Nothing made Jesus angrier (Luke 11:46).

Zophar's argument now takes an unexpected turn. Job 11:6 could be translated, 'You should acknowledge that God carries some of your waywardness for you' (Goldingay). Does Zophar know what he is saying? It contradicts his own arguments. Here is a fresh expression of God's ways in Job's story. Rather than an inflexible judge imposing rewards or punishments, Zophar suggests God is sharing Job's burdens. More completely than Zophar or Job yet know, Jesus reveals to us a God who does exactly this.

Lord, thank you for sharing my burdens, more deeply than I know.

DAVID RUNCORN

Job's redeemer

[Job said] 'O that my words were written down! O that they were inscribed in a book! O that with an iron pen and with lead they were engraved on a rock for ever! For I know that my Redeemer lives, and that at the last he will stand upon the earth; and after my skin has been thus destroyed, then in my flesh I shall see God, whom I shall see on my side, and my eyes shall behold, and not another. My heart faints within me!

Job begs his friends to stop tormenting him. Their long speeches are wearing him out. He has had enough. If no one around him believes him, then let someone take his story and chisel it in stone so it will not be lost and others who come after may read it. We are doing exactly that.

'For I know that my Redeemer lives' (v. 25). We come to the words made famous by Handel's *Messiah* and often assumed to apply to Jesus. In fact, the New Testament never makes this link explicit and Job is not actually referring to the Messiah here. The figure of the redeemer Job is speaking of cannot be closely paralleled with Jesus, though the temptation to seek this connection is understandable. A redeemer in Hebrew society was someone who could buy back a family member or act as an advocate on his or her behalf in a way the person concerned could not. Job seems convinced that somewhere on earth or even in the heavens, there is someone who will do this for him. We know no more than this. To this stubborn hope he clings—that a true testimony to his faith in God will endure, even if he himself does not ('away from my flesh' is the more accurate translation of verse 26).

I think of people today in the world who are suffering dreadfully, undefended against violence and evil, pleading their cause to no avail. Perhaps this is their prayer, too—that their story will not go untold and death itself will not leave them without a witness?

Lord, I pray for those whose story of faith and endurance
is known only to you.

DAVID RUNCORN

Bildad speaks

Then Bildad the Shuhite answered: 'Dominion and fear are with God... How then can a mortal be righteous before God? How can one born of woman be pure? If even the moon is not bright and the stars are not pure in his sight, how much less a mortal, who is a maggot, and a human being, who is a worm!' Then Job answered: 'How you have helped one who has no power! How you have assisted the arm that has no strength! How you have counselled one who has no wisdom, and given much good advice!'

I have friends whose son was born with a significant disability. At the time, they were attending a church of lively and confident faith, but they recall how difficult some in that community found the presence of their child. Perhaps his disability unsettled a community that believed faith was about healing and wholeness. It was hard to cope when prayers did not visibly change the situation. One commentator with a similar personal story to tell suggests that Bildad's response to Job represents the way people's stories and struggles can make others insecure in their faith.

Like Job's other friends, Bildad believes there must be a reason for this having happened. This is a moral universe. He is as confident in declaring God's judgment as he is God's blessing. If his sons died, he tells Job, it would be God's doing because they had sinned (8:4). The 'answers' that have secured Bildad in his faith and life, do not fit the questions Job's continuing struggles are throwing up, however. Bildad angrily confronts Job for not listening to his friend's advice, but it is not Job's job to make his counsellors feel good about themselves. After all, he is the one who has to live with all this. Bildad's anger is a symptom of how insecure he feels in the face of inexplicable suffering.

So, Job's reply to Bildad in today's passage is tough to hear, but wholly reasonable: 'nothing you are saying is helping me.'

Lord, help me let go of my need for security and truly be with others in what they are going through. Amen

DAVID RUNCORN

The days that are ours

'A mortal, born of woman, few of days and full of trouble, comes up like a flower and withers, flees like a shadow and does not last... Since their days are determined, and the number of their months is known to you, and you have appointed the bounds that they cannot pass, look away from them, and desist, that they may enjoy, like labourers, their days.'

These words are similar to those in Isaiah 40:6–8, which is traditionally read at funerals. Life is fleeting. That is why, according to an ancient tradition, Christians are marked with dust on Ash Wednesday with the words, 'Remember you are dust'. Much more than a sign of our sinfulness, it is a reminder of our mortality.

Life is a fleeting thing. It may be our unwillingness to accept this deepest truth about ourselves that is the source of so much of our wayward thinking and acting. Job asks why God does not leave such fragile creatures alone. Why not just leave us to enjoy the time that is ours? Like a worker with a job to do, at least let us have the satisfaction of finishing it. Instead, for Job, his life has become one of torment.

Have you ever wished God would pay you less attention, because the way of faith and trust feels like it is just too demanding? A psalm that expresses very similar thoughts to Job's concludes by saying to God, 'For I am your passing guest, an alien, like all my forebears. Turn your gaze away from me, that I may smile again, before I depart and am no more' (Psalm 39:12–13).

That life can be a trial we can barely cope with is a fact. That God can be addressed out of that despair is good news. There is somewhere to take our cries and prayers. Our business is with God. God is willing to hear and receive even our rawest responses. That Job addresses God in this way is a sign of faith, not the absence of it.

Lord, I pray for when life and faith leave me wearied,
unable to cope and I just want to be left alone. Amen

DAVID RUNCORN

God and the wild things

'Look at Behemoth, which I made just as I made you... its strength... and its power... It is the first of the great acts of God—only its Maker can approach it with the sword... Can you draw out Leviathan with a fish-hook... Will it speak soft words to you?... Will you play with it as with a bird...? Lay hands on it; think of the battle; you will not do it again!... Who can confront it and be safe?—under the whole heaven, who?... Its breath kindles coals, and a flame comes out of its mouth. In its neck abides strength, and terror dances before it.'

After revealing himself as the one who creates and orders this world, God now points out two creatures to Job: Behemoth and Leviathan. They are wild and frighteningly powerful. He teases Job, asking if he could he ever tame them.

God clearly finds them very exciting and boasts of them, calling them the first of his 'great acts' (v. 19). In that ancient world, Leviathan and Behemoth were semi-mythic creatures, representing the more chaotic and threatening elements in creation, where things can seem frighteningly out of control. A world with such creatures in it will certainly be unpredictable and dangerous at times, but God celebrates them and their presence.

In the Bible, there are times when God acts to limit or defeat these creatures (Psalms 12 and 74), but never wholly remove them. If this unruly wildness is not allowed to bring an end to life, neither is 'order' allowed to render it entirely safe and predictable. It is within the tension between the two that we find our freedom to choose, explore and take risks in life.

Where is the challenge for you in this? A God who allows wildness to roam in his world is surely not interested in simply telling us what to do. All too often, organised religion can feel like that. Richard Holloway once observed that, 'so much religion is an attempt to tame the madness of God'. So, what if faithful believing is invited to be as wild as it is ordered?

Lord, draw me to the wildness of life as much as to its ordering. Amen

DAVID RUNCORN

Out of the whirlwind

The Lord answered Job out of the whirlwind: 'Who is this that darkens counsel by words without knowledge? Gird up your loins like a man, I will question you... 'Where were you when I laid the foundation of the earth... when the morning stars sang together?... Have you commanded the morning since your days began?... Can you hunt the prey for the lion... ? Who provides for the raven its prey, when its young ones cry to God?'

It is worth reading from chapter 38 to 41 in one sweep. The beauty, power and vision are breathtaking, but do you find God's opening words to Job rather harsh? Perhaps they are thus out of tough but loving necessity, for God makes it very clear that we human beings are not the centre of this world. Nor is life organised around our needs and preferences—not even one special person's acute suffering. Job must de-centre his understanding. If there is an answer to all that is happening, it will only be found by being part of something bigger.

God is not telling Job that everything else is more important than him. He is not saying, 'You are way down the list of my priorities'. He is shocking Job into an awareness of a much bigger story. Job needs to hear this more, not less, in his questioning. When suffering and trials preoccupy us, the world easily shrinks around our own concerns and what is happening to us. In our struggles, we can become very self-absorbed—my pain, my need, my questions, my God caring for me. It can leave us very self-centred.

One of the puzzles about God in this poem is how he has not expressed compassion or concern for Job and what is going through, but here a curtain is drawn back. Far more than his power, this glorious celebration reveals God's continuous, imaginative, intimate involvement with all he has made, greatest to least. Nothing is outside his awareness or vision. What God creates he also sustains and in this truth lies Job's hope—and ours.

Lord, I am not the centre of the universe. Help me look beyond myself and find my place in something amazingly bigger. Amen

DAVID RUNCORN

Wondering and despising

Then Job answered the Lord: 'I have uttered what I did not understand, things too wonderful for me, which I did not know... I had heard of you by the hearing of the ear, but now my eye sees you; therefore I despise myself, and repent in dust and ashes.'... And the Lord restored the fortunes of Job when he had prayed for his friends; and the Lord gave Job twice as much as he had before... After this Job lived for one hundred and forty years, and saw his children, and his children's children, four generations. And Job died, old and full of days.

The final chapter of Job could sound like the happy ending of a Hollywood film of this story. Job is healed. His friends are rebuked. He is vindicated and now has double the abundance he had before. For readers whose struggles continue, this is often the hardest part of the story to hear. Also, does it not contradict what has gone before?

Although the narrator says he was 'restored', there are now two words in Job's life that were not there at the beginning: 'wonder' and 'despising'. They are connected.

Job has not actually received any answers. The problem suffering poses has not been solved. Instead, there is an air of humbled astonishment. Having stumbled out of long dark night of suffering, he is willingly surrendering himself, his narrow concerns and presumptuous claims to understanding to a God who is beyond all knowing. His life is now, quite literally, wonder-full.

What of the despising? It is a severe word and perilously easy to misunderstand. Job is not rejecting himself. Neither should we. Like Paul after his conversion, he despises or rejects his previous way of understanding himself and God. How could he have ever presumed so much? The glory lies in not knowing and yet trusting.

Job has not returned to his old life. There is no way back. He has emerged into a renewed one and at its heart is surrender and wonder before the God who honours those who honour him (1 Samuel 2:30).

Lord, bring me, with Job, to life that is wonder-full. Amen

DAVID RUNCORN

Calling

I wonder what your reaction is when someone mentions his or her 'calling' or 'vocation' and if you react in a different way to each word? The term 'vocation' comes simply from the Latin *vocare* meaning 'to call', so they both effectively mean the same thing, but they can be loaded with very different expectations. It is easy to believe that a vocation is something especially holy—becoming a nun or a priest, for example—or a demanding career based on dedication and sacrifice, such as becoming a teacher or nurse. A calling, in contrast, can seem a little more achievable. 'Are you called to do this?' some Christian friends might ask if we are considering setting up a new church initiative or moving house or making a lifestyle change.

The notes below show that whether you refer to a 'calling' or 'vocation', there is a long scriptural history of God reaching out to men and women of all ages and all backgrounds in order to ask something of them. What this 'something' is can vary. Sometimes it is a specific task, sometimes changing behaviour or an openness to new possibilities. It can be to an individual, a number of people or a whole nation. It can be for a big purpose or something apparently insignificant. All that is required is the answer, 'Yes'.

In my role as a Director of Ordinands, it is my privilege to work alongside people who believe that they are called to ordained ministry. Some of them will become priests for the remainder of their lives; others may discover that God is actually asking something else of them. It can take courage to pursue a vocation, whatever it turns out to be, but the journey can be exciting and fulfilling, too. God is able to use the people we are if we offer ourselves in service. If we call ourselves disciples of Christ, we need to listen out for God's call and be prepared to follow wherever it may lead.

AMANDA BLOOR

The nature of God

But Moses said to God, 'If I come to the Israelites and say to them, "The God of your ancestors has sent me to you", and they ask me, "What is his name?" what shall I say to them?' God said to Moses, 'I AM WHO I AM.'

Moses does not seek attention from God or long to be called into service. He is not perfect or even particularly devout. Nevertheless, he is asked by God to undertake a seemingly impossible task—lead the Israelites from slavery and suffering to a new home. Uncertain, Moses asks for proof of this calling. By taking back God's hidden name to his people, he hopes to convince them that they have found divine favour and will not be alone in their struggles for freedom. He wants authority, a sort of divine passport identifying himself as God's chosen servant. Instead, he is given insight into the very nature of God. The words translated here as 'I AM WHO I AM' can also mean 'I WILL BE WHO I WILL BE'—a dynamic self-identification that suggests endless possibility and requires a similarly active response.

It is easy, in an ever-changing world, to long for order and certainty. We might decide to offer our lives to God and live out our vocation, but, at heart, we would often prefer it if that calling were neatly packaged up, predictable and straightforward. If there were a clear plan and a definitive timetable, we could decide whether or not to step forward. This is not God's way. The God who says to Moses, 'I WILL BE WHO I WILL BE' asks that we commit to the unknown future and be who we will need to be.

Whether we view this as exhilarating freedom or terrifying responsibility depends on our nature, but one thing is sure, God will be with us. Then, everything is possible.

Do we trust God enough to offer our lives in service,
even if we are uncertain of where that will take us?

AMANDA BLOOR

The work continues

The Lord said to Moses, 'Take Joshua son of Nun, a man in whom is the spirit, and lay your hand upon him; have him stand before Eleazar the priest and all the congregation, and commission him in their sight. You shall give him some of your authority, so that all the congregation of the Israelites may obey.'

When God lets him know that his death is approaching, Moses is concerned for the future of the people he has led towards the Promised Land. How will they manage without his guiding influence? Who will be their shepherd when he is no longer with them?

Moses has no need to be anxious; God is able to provide a successor. In a ritual that remains familiar to us today, Joshua is called out for a particular ministry, gifted with God's spirit of wisdom and presented to the congregation. He is publicly commissioned for the task asked of him, hands are laid on him in prayer and he works for a while alongside the more experienced man.

It is a good reminder that any form of authorised Christian ministry is undertaken with the agreement of the gathered community, the authority of those in religious leadership and—most importantly—in God's strength and with God's guidance. Joshua's calling is not to be a second Moses, however. He will learn from his forefather in faith, but his role will be different, reflecting the changing situation and utilising his own unique gifts and skills. God knows what is needed and who will be best for the task. All that is necessary is for Joshua to trust, respond, be brave and faithful. God will be with him in what is to come.

The lives and work of other Christians can be an example and an inspiration, but it is important to remember that God calls us as we are. We cannot replicate other people's vocations, but we can, with God's help, live out our own.

AMANDA BLOOR

Fear and doubt

At that time Deborah, a prophetess, wife of Lappidoth, was judging Israel. She used to sit under the palm of Deborah between Ramah and Bethel in the hill country of Ephraim; and the Israelites came up to her for judgement. She sent and summoned Barak son of Abinoam from Kedesh in Naphtali and said to him, 'The Lord, the God of Israel, commands you, "Go, take position at Mount Tabor."'

Deborah was a prophet and judge. Sitting in a public space she offers leadership, dispensing advice to those who seek her out. She is influential enough to summon Barak, a military leader, into her presence and tell him what his strategy against Israel's enemies should be. Barak appears suspicious—perhaps because she is a woman and, he probably thinks, does not understand such things or he has come across untrustworthy prophets before—and has a cunning response. 'Come with me,' he says, 'and I will do what you suggest.' The sub-text is clear: if Deborah really is relaying God's orders, then she will not hesitate. If she refuses, then her words must be false.

It is a battle of wits that Deborah appears to relish. She calmly points out that if she goes with Barak into battle, any success will be ascribed to her rather than gaining glory for him. Some 10,000 Israelite warriors then face the Canaanite forces and it is Deborah's encouragement that propels them to successful action. Sisera, fleeing to safety, is put bloodily to death by another woman, Jael, and the Israelites are victorious.

We may be surprised by the actions of the two strong women in this story, although the matter-of-fact way in which it is reported suggests that female leadership and action were not uncommon in ancient Israel. Barak's reluctance to act on Deborah's prophecy is understandable, however. How is he to know that she is telling the truth and that her words are really from God? That is a question we face, too. How do we discern what is from God and when does fear inhibit our response?

Prayer, study of scripture and the wisdom of the community of faith can all help us to discern God's calling. Who would you turn to for prayerful advice?

AMANDA BLOOR

Love and affection

Ruth said: 'Do not press me to leave you or to turn back from following you! Where you go, I will go; where you lodge, I will lodge; your people shall be my people, and your God my God.'

Imagine the grief that Naomi must have felt when both her sons died within a short period of time. There must also have been concern as she had been widowed some years earlier and now there were no men in the household to take care of her in her old age. Bravely setting her two daughters-in-law free to go and find new husbands, she expected to be alone for the rest of her life.

Ruth refuses to leave her, however. In a touching and emotional outburst, she vows to remain with Naomi wherever she goes, even follow her mother-in-law's faith. They will, together, become a new family. Thus, the two women travel to Bethlehem, Naomi's home town, and a train of events is set in motion that will lead to marriage and the birth of a son, Obed. Obed will be the father of Jesse and Jesse will be the father of King David—a royal line that will in time lead to a small stable in Bethlehem where Joseph will hold his own newborn son and name him Jesus.

Ruth was not called on to undertake a particular task. There are no burning bushes or angelic messengers. God does not speak to her directly, but, under the guidance of the older woman and held within Naomi's faith, she becomes part of God's plan. Building family life, in all its variety, is a vocation and Ruth's future is shaped by her willingness to act lovingly towards Naomi and the affection each woman bears for the other. It is their relationship that allows trust to grow and out of that trust, God's blessing is bestowed on them and the world.

The example and encouragement of those we love and who love us can be enormously influential. Give thanks today for someone who has helped to shape and grow your faith.

AMANDA BLOOR

A calling has no barriers

Samuel was lying down in the temple of the Lord, where the ark of God was. Then the Lord called, 'Samuel! Samuel!' and he said, 'Here I am!' and ran to Eli, and said, 'Here I am, for you called me.' But he said, 'I did not call; lie down again.'

How old do you have to be to be called by God? It is a question to which the Church has not always had a clear answer. Until fairly recently, it was common for young applicants to ordained or other ministries to be told to go away and get some life experience first. That can feel like rejection and be enough to stifle, at least for a while, a deeply held vocation.

The story of the child Samuel reminds us that God does not set barriers on a calling. Age, gender, race, position, education—all are irrelevant when God intervenes. Offered to God's service by his grateful parents, ministering in the Temple alongside Eli the priest, Samuel was only a young boy, yet God called out to him. There were tasks he wanted him to undertake.

At first, Samuel assumed that it was Eli who had called out in the night. Eli assumed that Samuel was imagining a voice in his sleep. Yet, God was persistent and the calling continued until it was answered. 'Speak, Lord,' said Samuel, 'for your servant is listening' (v. 9) and God spoke.

Samuel went on to become one of the greatest of the prophets and a wise judge over Israel. He grew in stature with maturity, yet, as a child, he was tasked with delivering a difficult message to Eli. Even at that first moment of God's calling, Samuel was trusted to do what was asked of him and, with Eli's encouragement, he was able to respond to God with openness and trust. Can we react with similar confidence that God will be with us in whatever we are called to do in Christian service?

Eli helped Samuel to believe that God really was calling him.
Pray that each of us can be ready to not only hear God's voice in
our own lives but also encourage others to listen and respond.

AMANDA BLOOR

God will not be confined

That same night the word of the Lord came to Nathan, saying: Go and tell my servant David: Thus says the Lord: You shall not build me a house to live in. For I have not lived in a house since the day I brought out Israel to this very day, but I have lived in a tent and a tabernacle.

What would be more seemly than to create a place of beauty in which to worship God? David has cemented his role as king by moving into a palace of cedar wood, created by fine craftsmen. He now wishes to create something of similar splendour in which to house the ark of the covenant.

The prophet Nathan tells David that God refuses to be confined in a house of cedar. The people of Israel have been on the move for generations and God has journeyed with them. Now is the time to not make a fine temple but create an established and settled kingdom. It will be his son Solomon, not David, who builds the Temple in Jerusalem that will become the focus for Jewish devotions.

It seems axiomatic that God deserves our very best and, for some, this has meant building beautiful churches filled with precious ornamentation and artwork. Others have sought God in places of quiet simplicity and there have been times throughout the centuries when this diversity of spiritual expression has caused division. We might react in shock to the destruction of historic monuments in today's troubled Near East, but it has happened much closer to home, too. The defaced monuments in many English parish churches recall the iconoclasts of the Reformation and conflicts between historical expression and contemporaneous belief.

God's rejection of David's plans for a temple reminds us that religious buildings should be for God's glory rather than ours. More than that, the story is an affirmation of the fact that we follow a God who is not to be shut away safely in a building, however glorious. God roams free and calls to people outside the church as well as within it.

Help us, O God, to look for signs of your presence in the wider world and the people we will meet today. Amen

AMANDA BLOOR

God uses people, places and situations

Mordecai told them to reply to Esther, 'Do not think that in the king's palace you will escape any more than all the other Jews. For if you keep silence at such a time as this, relief and deliverance will rise for the Jews from another quarter, but you and your father's family will perish. Who knows? Perhaps you have come to royal dignity for just such a time as this.'

Being the consort of a powerful and autocratic man can be dangerous. King Ahasuerus has already cast aside one wife because she refused his drunken command, so Esther—chosen to be queen because of her youthful beauty—knows that her life is subject to her husband's whims. Yet, she is called on to put herself in danger in an attempt to save her people from destruction.

Mordecai urges Esther to act because she is the only one who is in a position to influence the king for good. Perhaps, he muses, her rise to royal status has been for precisely this purpose. She is the right person in the right place at the right time and she can make a real difference. Esther agrees to help, but does not act until she, her maids and all of the Jewish population of the city have prepared themselves by prayer and fasting. They are God's people and they act devoutly.

While we hope that most of us will never be called to make life or death decisions, there will be many moments in our lives when we are faced with choices that will have consequences. Is God speaking to us in those moments? Can we have the courage to do the right thing, even if it is difficult? If we bring God into our decisionmaking, then even the messiest moments have the potential to be used for good.

Identify a person in Christian history or your own experience who acted faithfully in response to God's calling and consider what their example says to you.

AMANDA BLOOR

God is in the darkness

But you, O Lord, reign for ever; your throne endures to all generations. Why have you forgotten us completely? Why have you forsaken us these many days? Restore us to yourself, O Lord, that we may be restored; renew our days as of old—unless you have utterly rejected us, and are angry with us beyond measure.

So much of our theology talks about the good news offered by faith that it can sometimes be hard to deal with distress and disappointment. Yet, this was repeatedly the experience of the Jewish people, who found themselves in slavery, exile, oppressed by the powerful and mourning the destruction of their cities and holy places. This passage from Lamentations gives voice to the bewilderment that afflicted them when things went so badly wrong. 'Why has this happened? Has God forgotten us? Have we been so wicked that God has turned away from us completely? Are we being punished?'

Unless we have a theology that can address times of failure, there is danger we will fall into despair. It is easy to believe when things are going well and think we are being rewarded in some way for our faith and our devotion, that we deserve good things and God favours us over others. If we begin to view God as an indulgent parent playing favourites, however, that false image of God can quickly turn into one of a tyrant who is angry, disappointed and distant. This can threaten and undermine our faith.

It is good to remember that we are called to follow Christ—and Christ himself, so close to God that he knew him as 'Father'—understood what it was to feel rejected and alone. Indeed, abandoned by his friends, hanging in agony on the cross, Jesus cried out in bewilderment, 'My God, my God, why have you forsaken me?' (Matthew 27:46). He found he was not alone, however, and his glorious resurrection followed this apparent disaster. God never wishes suffering on us and is always with us in times of trouble as well as in moments of joy.

Pray for all those who are suffering today, especially those whose faith is under strain or have no faith to sustain them.

AMANDA BLOOR

A calling and the community

'Come, let us return to the Lord; for it is he who has torn, and he will heal us; he has struck down, and he will bind us up. After two days he will revive us; on the third day he will raise us up, that we may live before him. Let us know, let us press on to know the Lord.'

A vocation can involve an individual in a task that at first seems endless or impossible. In this passage, we are reminded that Hosea the prophet's calling is to bring a whole people back to faith and to a Godly way of living. They have followed other gods and turned away from the religious practices of their ancestors; their future looks bleak. Yet Hosea is tasked with reminding them of God's faithfulness so that they may ask for forgiveness, be freed from their guilt, and once again flourish.

It's a huge thing to ask of one man. Yet we need to remember that as Hosea's words begin to impact upon his listeners, the few who are encouraged will influence others and they in turn will have an effect upon many more. Like a wave building in amplitude as it reaches the shore, what begins as a small advance will eventually have the power to move multitudes.

We can probably recognise, if we look back, incidents in history when what began as a small act of bravery or resistance was picked up by many people and led to immense political change. The fall of the Berlin Wall and the collapse of communism in Eastern Europe was one such moment. However, less dramatic occurrences can still be hugely significant. Churches have through the centuries been places of refuge, offering support to the weak and fighting for justice for the oppressed. This task continues today, as refugees flee from war-torn countries and the poor look for practical support. As individuals we are called by God to make a difference; as communities of faith we can begin to change the world.

What does your church or congregation do when called upon to aid those who need help?

AMANDA BLOOR

Follow me and fish

As he walked by the Sea of Galilee, he saw two brothers, Simon, who is called Peter, and Andrew his brother, casting a net into the lake—for they were fishermen. And he said to them, 'Follow me, and I will make you fish for people.' Immediately they left their nets and followed him.

When we talk about a vocation, we often think of only one thing: the ordained ministry. Yet, God calls people to all sorts of ways of living out their faith, a whole variety of ministries. Each is important and each allows these individuals to use the gifts and skills they already possess. Instead of trying to be something completely new, they are enabled to be more fully the people God knows they are.

We see this in the most famous of the accounts of people being called in the Bible. Simon and Andrew are going about their daily business of catching fish. Jesus calls them to follow him and they respond immediately, leaving their nets and heading with him into a new future.

There are many elements in this short passage that are of importance: Jesus' authority and charisma, which mean that he simply says 'come' and strangers respond to him; the faith shown by Simon Peter and Andrew, who trust and follow; the fact that they are called to something that builds on the things they already know. Jesus does not ask them to follow him and become great theologians or church treasurers; he says simply, come and 'fish for people' (v. 19). They are to use what they already are in God's service.

God knows us through and through and promises to be with us throughout our lives. If we respond to God's calling, we should trust that we will be enabled to do something that fits with who we already are. We do not have to become someone else.

Consider some of the Christians you know well and think about the gifts they use for the Church and others. Help them to recognise these as vocations. What might your own calling be?

AMANDA BLOOR

Supporting one another

The Lord appointed seventy others and sent them on ahead of him in pairs to every town and place where he himself intended to go. He said to them, 'The harvest is plentiful, but the labourers are few; therefore ask the Lord of the harvest to send out labourers into his harvest. Go on your way.'

It can sometimes feel isolating to recognise a vocation or calling. Simply acknowledging that God might be asking something of us is hard enough; to share this belief with others can be difficult, especially in the early stages. It is easy to wonder if we are imagining God's calling and fear that people will think we are looking for attention or recognition. We can feel inadequate and unworthy. We can wonder how, if it is even slightly possible that we are called, we will ever be able to do what is required.

This is nothing new! Jesus understood that stepping out in faith is difficult and to do it alone would be almost impossible. Even when we hear him acknowledging that there are only a few labourers to gather in the plentiful harvest of souls, we see him pairing up the 70 he has appointed to go out ahead of him. They will travel together, ensuring that everyone has company, encouragement and support on the journey.

It is very rare to find someone called to live out a vocation that does not involve others. Even those living a vowed solitary life do this with the prayerful and practical support of a religious community. Yes, it is important for each of us to pray and reflect on what God might be asking of us, listening to that small interior voice, but it is crucial we do not try to make this journey alone. Vocations involve the whole Christian community.

Are our own communities of faith welcoming and encouraging about vocations? We can pray both that we and others will listen to God's call to us and we can be faithful supporters of people discerning what their own vocations may be.

AMANDA BLOOR

I chose you

'I have called you friends, because I have made known to you everything that I have heard from my Father. You did not choose me but I chose you. And I appointed you to go and bear fruit, fruit that will last, so that the Father will give you whatever you ask him in my name.'

This is rich in meaning and encouragement, summing up in a few apparently simple words the wonder of vocations. Jesus is nearing the end of his earthly ministry. The Last Supper has just taken place, Judas has slipped out of the upper room to betray his master and the remaining disciples are anxious that Christ's words are about leaving them to go where they cannot yet follow. In response, he talks to them about love and trust, promising that ,when he goes away, the Holy Spirit will be given to them so they will not be alone.

Then Jesus says the words quoted above. 'I have called you friends', he tells the disciples—they are not his servants—and so he has told them 'everything' (v. 15). He chose them to be close to him and is asking them to, with God's help, go out and continue the task that they started.

Those words echo down the centuries to challenge and inspire all those who call themselves Christians. Each of us is called to follow Christ, not as a servant, but—astoundingly—as a trusted friend. Each of us is known so intimately that it is Christ who chooses us, not we who decide to draw close to him. Each of us has a job to do: we are to bear fruit that will last.

'I chose you' (v. 16) No longer can we hide behind the excuse that we are not the right person, not good enough, not ready for this. Christ has chosen us to be entrusted with a particular task.

'I chose you.' This is a direct appeal. Jesus is saying, 'You have been chosen for this.' How can we turn away?

Your vocation will be personal to you, using your experience, your gifts, your skills and your desires. Pray today for grace to hear God's calling and respond with joy and trust, certain of Jesus' friendship and support.

AMANDA BLOOR

Christmas

Matthew's Gospel has a broad and ambitious focus. It sets out to tell the story of Jesus as a gift to the whole world. For Matthew, the gift is this: that Jesus is Emmanuel—God with us. This revelation, close to the beginning of the Gospel, sets the tone for the whole piece. Everything from this point onwards needs to be read or heard with the hope of God-with-us in view. Everything that Jesus does or says, asks or teaches is an insight into the nature of God.

The Nativity story as told in Matthew shows no interest in the details of Jesus' birth or the 'Holy Night' (we need to go to the brilliant storytelling in the Gospel of Luke for that). Instead, Matthew's focus is on how the birth came about and its ramifications, for both the Holy Family and the wider world. So, attention if paid to the place of Jesus in the history of the Jewish people. There is a particular focus on the decisions that Joseph and Mary have to make and how they make them. The Gospel writer understands them to be exemplars of all that is required in people of faith. For Matthew, the angelic visitations provide guidance and reassurance and the mysterious 'wise men from the East' (2:1) play a vital role in Matthew's telling of the story. Their faith, from beyond the boundaries of the Jewish religious tradition, is a sign that this Jesus is a gift to all and may be recognised and welcomed as such.

At the end of Matthew's Gospel, we are returned to the theme of God-with-us. On the mountain, the disciples are commissioned by the risen Jesus to go into all the world and make disciples of all nations. Their commissioning and the Gospel close with Jesus' words: 'And remember. I am with you always' (28:20). With the disciples, we are called to live in the joyful revelation of God-with-us, to live and share the great story of Emmanuel.

May you be blessed this Christmas and may you carry the hope of God-with-us wherever you are, wherever you go. Grace and peace to you.

IAN ADAMS

'Do not be afraid'

Now the birth of Jesus the Messiah took place in this way. When his mother Mary had been engaged to Joseph, but before they lived together, she was found to be with child from the Holy Spirit. Her husband Joseph, being a righteous man and unwilling to expose her to public disgrace, planned to dismiss her quietly. But just when he had resolved to do this, an angel of the Lord appeared to him in a dream and said, 'Joseph, son of David, do not be afraid to take Mary as your wife, for the child conceived in her is from the Holy Spirit. She will bear a son, and you are to name him Jesus, for he will save his people from their sins.'

In Matthew's Gospel, the Jesus story begins and ends with the same message of reassurance. In a dream (a theme to which we will return later in these notes), Joseph encounters an angel of the Lord. 'Do not be afraid' (v. 20) is almost the first thing that the angel says (understandably perhaps!) Towards the end of the Gospel, both an angel and then the risen Jesus himself will greet Mary Magdalene and the other Mary with the same words. In both circumstances, those receiving the words of reassurance are not only having to work out how to be in the company of a heavenly being but also how to engage with the seemingly impossible.

Whether you are facing the impossible at this time or perhaps just coping with the usual demands of life, it is interesting (if not a little humiliating) to reflect on how much we can be driven—or immobilised—by fear. Lots of things are, of course, beyond our control. Fear comes with being human in an unpredictable world. We should not try to deny it or defeat it, but fear can be dealt with and we need not be shaped by it. At the heart of the nativity story is the message that, in God's care, we need not be fearful.

Of what are you fearful at this time? May the words of the angel be a gift for you today: 'Do not be afraid' (v. 20).

IAN ADAMS

Emmanuel—God with us

All this took place to fulfil what had been spoken by the Lord through the prophet: 'Look, the virgin shall conceive and bear a son, and they shall name him Emmanuel,' which means, 'God is with us.' When Joseph awoke from sleep, he did as the angel of the Lord commanded him; he took her as his wife, but had no marital relations with her until she had borne a son; and he named him Jesus.

Let us not miss the wonder of what is about to happen. God with us. God as one of us. God alongside us. God deep within the experience of being human. In the holy child, God comes to our touch, sight and hearing. We can hear God breathing, crying and, in time, laughing and talking. God is as close as it gets!

Let us not miss the wonder, too, of what is about to happen on a cosmic scale. The Nativity story reveals that God's Holy Spirit is at work across time and space, always imagining a new future. In the Nativity story a young woman is 'with child from the Holy Spirit' (v. 18). Who knows what is being conceived and brought to birth as you are reading this?

It is easy for us now to read back into the Christmas story an inevitably happy outcome. We celebrate the joy and wonder of Christ's birth every year, but this wondrous outcome was, of course, not nearly so obvious for Joseph and Mary.

Nevertheless, for Joseph, the revelation of God's presence through the angel inspires him to an act of great love and faith, taking Mary as his wife. He elects to put his reputation on the line and, perhaps, also his place in community and society. Joseph is, as Matthew has told us, a righteous man. Joseph has already encountered the presence of God within himself. Now, waking from his dream and inspired by the angel's invitation, Joseph (as Mary has already done) lets that presence shape his decision. The revelation of God-with-us has awakened new possibilities within him.

How might the revelation of God-with-us inspire you in a decision that you face at this time?

IAN ADAMS

Where is the child?

In the time of King Herod, after Jesus was born in Bethlehem of Judea, wise men from the East came to Jerusalem, asking, 'Where is the child who has been born king of the Jews? For we observed his star at its rising, and have come to pay him homage.' When King Herod heard this, he was frightened, and all Jerusalem with him; and calling together all the chief priests and scribes of the people, he inquired of them where the Messiah was to be born. They told him, 'In Bethlehem of Judea; for so it has been written by the prophet: "And you, Bethlehem, in the land of Judah, are by no means least among the rulers of Judah; for from you shall come a ruler who is to shepherd my people Israel."'

It is Christmas! The Nativity, the birth of the holy child. May you be blessed on this great and wonderful day.

In Matthew's telling of the story, 'wise men from the East' (v. 1) have followed a star at its rising. And if ever there was a night and day to look up in wonder, this was it. The question on the lips of the curious and faithful wise men may be a gift to us, a question that we can carry through this day and the Christmas season: 'Where is the child… ?' (v. 2).

One insight in response to this question is that the child may be found in unexpected places, in out-of-the-way settings and out-of-sight people. Even, perhaps, in us. Indeed, signs of the holy child may be found in every human being. Of course, such traces may seem more obvious in some people than others. Even on this holy day, you may encounter someone in whom such signs are hard to see. We cannot change that, but we can keep on searching. We can also give attention to how the holy child may be somehow, amazingly, perceived in us.

Jesus—holy child and God-with-us—on this Christmas day,
I devote myself again to you.

IAN ADAMS

Overwhelmed with joy

Then Herod secretly called for the wise men and learned from them the exact time when the star had appeared. Then he sent them to Bethlehem, saying, 'Go and search diligently for the child; and when you have found him, bring me word so that I may also go and pay him homage.' When they had heard the king, they set out; and there, ahead of them, went the star that they had seen at its rising, until it stopped over the place where the child was. When they saw that the star had stopped, they were overwhelmed with joy. On entering the house, they saw the child with Mary his mother; and they knelt down and paid him homage. Then, opening their treasure-chests, they offered him gifts of gold, frankincense, and myrrh. And having been warned in a dream not to return to Herod, they left for their own country by another road.

There is plenty in the world that can make us despondent. So, when something truly good emerges, it deserves our joyful response. We all have different ways of doing joy, ranging from expressions of quiet contentment to bursts of exuberant ecstasy. May you let the wonder of God-with-us overwhelm you with joy today, then let your joy evolve into thankfulness.

The wise men were able to express their joy with gifts of gold, frankincense and myrrh. These might not be the gifts that we have to hand, but how might our joy be expressed? The spirit of the wise men's gifts can be ours. If ever there was a moment for a thankful gesture of extravagance—a gift of gold—this perhaps is it. What a day on which to celebrate the presence of God-with-us with all the senses—a frankincense moment. In this season of birth, it may be important, too, to find a way to mark God's presence in death and beyond it—a gesture of myrrh. Later, Jesus will explain his desire 'that my joy may be in you, and that your joy may be complete' (John 15:11). A despondent world is reshaped by joy.

How might you express your joy and thankfulness today?

IAN ADAMS

Wonder, dream and angels

Now after they had left, an angel of the Lord appeared to Joseph in a dream and said, 'Get up, take the child and his mother, and flee to Egypt, and remain there until I tell you; for Herod is about to search for the child, to destroy him.' Then Joseph got up, took the child and his mother by night, and went to Egypt, and remained there until the death of Herod. This was to fulfil what had been spoken by the Lord through the prophet, 'Out of Egypt I have called my son.'

The Nativity story invites us to feel wonder. On occasion we may be called, with all of Matthew's readers and hearers over the centuries, into the realms of the extraordinary. For Matthew, the presence of angels is an integral element in the Nativity story. Mary had been asked by the Angel Gabriel to yield to the impossible possibility that she might become the bearer of God into the world. An angel of the Lord had then appeared to Joseph, reassuring him about Mary. Now, following the birth of Jesus, an angel warns Joseph to take the Holy Family to safety in Egypt.

In my own experience, dreams seem often to be baffling and incoherent—just the final chaotic sparks of one day's brain activity as it winds down, or the first noisy buzz of the new day's energy as the brain wakes back up again. Sometimes, however, our dreams may reveal more. Even though it is very occasionally, Matthew might suggest, angels may come.

Dreams may be common; lucid or memorable dreams are perhaps less so, and angelic encounters are very unusual. We cannot chase dreams, even less so angelic encounters, but we can nurture a quiet state of alertness to the presence of Emmanuel—of God-with-us and of God within us. We can give ourselves to the many wonders of daily life that, in God's grace, come our way and the wonder of God's creation surrounding us, full of divine life, even in winter.

---

*What might your dreams be revealing this Christmas season?
What is the wonder that you are noticing?*

IAN ADAMS

Lamentation

When Herod saw that he had been tricked by the wise men, he was infuriated, and he sent and killed all the children in and around Bethlehem who were two years old or under, according to the time that he had learned from the wise men. Then was fulfilled what had been spoken through the prophet Jeremiah: 'A voice was heard in Ramah, wailing and loud lamentation, Rachel weeping for her children; she refused to be consoled, because they are no more.'

In the celebratory season of Christmas, this day, known as Holy Innocents, comes as a shock, but it is important that it is remembered. It can be easy to overstate the extent of the bad things that happen around us and in the wider world, but truly terrible things do happen. Human beings do dehumanising things, perhaps as a result of some deep, if unrecognised, perception of not being loved or an instinct to transmit our pain to others rather than transform it into something more positive.

In Matthew's account, one of the great horrors of the New Testament period is described—the killing by Herod of the babies and young children of Bethlehem. In our own time, innocents continue to be abused and massacred. How do we react to such terrible events? We should, of course, strive to do whatever we can to ensure that they are not repeated, but we also need to lament.

Lamentation is one of the tough gifts of the Hebrew scriptures. The spaces they create for lament suggest that it is a practice that enables us to engage with what has happened and prepare ourselves to be involved in the shaping of a much better future. Lamentation is a key step along the path towards a better world.

For this to happen, we need to give ourselves to it—not rushing on to some supposedly happier place, but giving room for the lamentation to breathe. Then, in time, we can discover a measure of God's healing. As with joy, we all lament in different ways. However you do it, may you find the courage to enter the place of lament and discover the hope that will emerge.

What or whom are you lamenting today?

IAN ADAMS

Cave of the heart

When Herod died, an angel of the Lord suddenly appeared in a dream to Joseph in Egypt and said, 'Get up, take the child and his mother, and go to the land of Israel, for those who were seeking the child's life are dead.' Then Joseph got up, took the child and his mother, and went to the land of Israel. But when he heard that Archelaus was ruling over Judea in place of his father Herod, he was afraid to go there. And after being warned in a dream, he went away to the district of Galilee. There he made his home in a town called Nazareth, so that what had been spoken through the prophets might be fulfilled, 'He will be called a Nazorean.'

Time to go home. Once again, Joseph encounters an angel and a return home is planned. As the story unfolds in Matthew's account, it turns out that Nazareth will be the new family home.

We are all trying to find a place to call home. A place where we can be ourselves, that is a source of energy and restoration, a place where, as the Old Testament prophet Micah (4:4) put it, 'they shall all sit under their own vines and under their own fig trees, and no one shall make them afraid.' Such a home is the setting out of which we may bring our God-given goodness to the world.

Home is also located within us, wherever we are. This is home as the still centre within which we may discover both ourselves and God. It is the location of a life of prayer and the means to an ever-deepening sense of our union with God, a place where we come to realise that we are truly beloved by God. There is an Orthodox understanding of this still place as the cave of the heart. It is our true home and one that moves with us, wherever we go, wherever we are. It is also the place of belonging and becoming, through which all that the prophets have ever hoped for may be best fulfilled.

What does home mean to you? How might you nurture the still place home, the cave of the heart?

IAN ADAMS

Tough edge

In those days John the Baptist appeared in the wilderness of Judea, proclaiming, 'Repent, for the kingdom of heaven has come near.'

Christmas has a tough edge. For many it can be an extraordinarily demanding time. While some celebrate, many are simply trying to survive. To those of us with the privilege of being able to celebrate, the nativity story still brings tough questions, probing us to think about what really matters, and asking us to make changes.

As the nativity story concludes, Matthew introduces John the Baptist and makes explicit a link between John and Jesus. John's message, says Matthew, is a call to repentance, or change of heart and direction, and a proclamation that 'the kingdom of heaven has come near' (v. 2). As we read on in the Gospels, we soon realise that this coming kingdom is at the heart of Jesus' prophetic words and actions. For Jesus, God's rule of peace and justice is not only coming but is already beginning to be experienced around us, among us, even despite us.

As a result of the nativity of Jesus, Matthew seems to be saying, something has changed. In fact, everything has changed. The birth of Jesus has signalled the coming of God's kingdom. So, the wise men are kneeling before one whose small presence is changing history. This Emmanuel, this God-with-us is not only pointing to God's coming kingdom but also somehow bringing it into being. Every future word of Jesus, every gesture, every action and every encounter will be a reshaping of the world for good.

So, 'What,' Matthew might be asking of us, 'should be our response now?' In the spirit of John the Baptist, our response surely needs to involve a reassessment of our priorities, repentance regarding wrong orientations and a turning towards God and actions that may enable God's kingdom to flourish. If we allow it to do so, the tough edge of Christmas comes to individuals and communities, churches and institutions. 'Repent, for the kingdom of heaven has come near' (v. 2).

During this Christmas season, a new year nearly here, what do you sense may need to change?

IAN ADAMS

Preparing the way

This is the one of whom the prophet Isaiah spoke when he said, 'The voice of one crying out in the wilderness: "Prepare the way of the Lord, make his paths straight."'

We conclude these Christmas notes with a journey into the wilderness. This is when John the Baptist exercises his wild and prophetic ministry. It is when Jesus the man will begin his own public ministry. Matthew reaches back into the Jewish scriptures to make a link between the old and new prophets of the wilderness and suggests that both are pointing towards Jesus as God-with-us. The Lord that the old prophet Isaiah proclaimed is identified with the one to whom the new prophet John will point—Jesus the holy child of the Nativity become man. With one voice, both old and new prophets call on us to 'Prepare the way of the Lord' and 'make his paths straight' (v. 3) in the wilderness.

We are involved now in this task of way-preparing and path-straightening. We are called to share the person and the story of Christ in action and in word. Christmas is once a year, but the event—the incarnation of Christ—continues. The Nativity takes shape again and again, as Christ is born every day in his people. Each one of us is called to bear Christ into the world.

This calling is a great privilege, but it may feel like a wilderness experience. Not everyone will welcome Christ and his coming kingdom. There is a lot of suspicion and scepticism surrounding the Christian religion, but my experience is that, even if our religion is treated with caution, the holy child, Jesus, may still be accepted and even welcomed. Whenever Christ is borne by his followers into the world with love, humility and courage, things change for the better. God's way continues to be opened up, healing comes and the wilderness springs into new life.

What might be the wilderness that you face? In the coming New Year, how might you prepare the way of the Lord with love, humility and courage?

IAN ADAMS

This page is left blank for your notes.

Reading *New Daylight* in a group

SALLY WELCH

I am aware that although some of you cherish the moments of quiet during the day that enable you to read and reflect on the passages we offer you in *New Daylight*, other readers prefer to study in small groups, to enable conversation and discussion and the sharing of insights. With this in mind, here are some ideas for discussion starters within a study group. Some of the questions are generic and can be applied to any set of contributions within this issue; others are specific to certain sets of readings. I hope they generate some interesting reflections and conversations.

General discussion starters

These questions can be used for any study series within this issue. Remember, there are no right or wrong answers; they are intended simply to enable a group to engage in conversation.

- What do you think is the main idea or theme of the author in this series? Do you think the writer succeeded in communicating this idea to you, or were you more interested in the side issues?

- Have you had any experience of the issues that are raised in the study? How have they affected your life?

- What evidence does the author use to support their ideas? Do they use personal observations and experience, facts, or quotations from other authorities? Which appeals to you most?

- Does the author make a 'call to action'? Is that call realistic and achievable? Do you think their ideas will work in the secular world?

- Can you identify specific passages that struck you personally—as interesting, profound, difficult to understand or illuminating?

- Did you learn something new from reading this series? Will you think differently about some things, and if so, what are they?

Calling (Amanda Bloor)

Amanda explores the wide range of ways in which people were called in the Bible, and the equally diverse tasks to which they were called. What has God called you to do in your life? What is he calling you to today? How will you respond?

Revelation 1—4 (Veronica Zundel)

The book of Revelation is challenging and often confusing. Veronica helps us to understand the book not as a prediction of future events but as a way of understanding the present, revealing its realities. 'A prophet is a person who accurately predicts the present,' she writes. How is this statement true? Is there value in prophets today? In what ways should we be prophets within our own communities?

Reflective question: The Psalms of Ascent by David Winter

In his exploration of this group of Psalms—sung, it is believed, by pilgrims to Jerusalem as they approached that most holy of places, the temple—David invites us to reflect on our relationship with God and with each other as we worship together.

'Wherever God's people meet is holy ground.' What does this mean to you as you come to worship each week? What makes you more aware of the presence of God in your worship—the place where you meet or the people you meet with?

Author profile: Amanda Bloor

Revd Amanda Bloor is a new contributor to *New Daylight* this year. Editor **Sally Welch** asked her to talk about her work and her writing.

How long have you been an Anglican priest, and what first inspired you to seek ordination?

I was ordained deacon in 2004 and priest in 2005. It wasn't part of my life-plan, but I'd taken a year out of work to study and reflect upon the future, and God got in there! To my surprise, I discovered that I was being asked to be ordained, and the journey began.

You work with the Armed Forces. Can you describe what your job involves?

I've had contact with the Armed Forces for most of my adult life and I'm currently a chaplain to the Army Cadet Force (a uniformed youth organisation). This can involve anything from responding to homesickness at Annual Camp or offering pastoral support to a young person, to leading a Drumhead Service for 250 non-churchgoers, answering questions about faith, ethics and morality. It's challenging, rewarding and fun.

You say you enjoy reading feminist theology. Can you explain a little more about that?

How long do you have? A good starting point is to look at faith, scripture, tradition and experience from a female point of view and ask if that opens up any new understandings.

How are you finding the experience of writing Bible reading notes?

I love the challenge of wrestling with a text and seeing it in a new way, then trying to say something that's relevant and engaging to a wider audience.

Which spiritual writers have influenced you and in what ways?

I've been influenced by St Benedict's common sense mixed with his deep love of humanity, the wisdom and faith of Julian of Norwich, Elizabeth Schüssler Fiorenza for daring to say challenging things drawn from careful intellectual investigation, and Kathleen Norris for putting spirituality into contemporary lived experience.

Do you have an unfulfilled wish or ambition?

Lots! I'd like to write a novel, travel widely, meet new people, finally learn to play the guitar... I could go on! There are so many adventures ahead.

What would you like your headstone to say?

'Wife, mother, priest.' That sums it up, really—a series of vocations, each one leading to the next. As simple as that.

Recommended reading

ESTHER TAYLOR

Lighted Windows
An Advent calendar for a world in waiting

MARGARET SILF

pb, 9780857464323, £7.99

From the bestselling author Margaret Silf, *Lighted Windows* (revised and updated since its first edition in 2002) offers readings, reflections and prayers or points for meditation for every day from 1 December to 6 January (Epiphany). The book is based on the theme of looking through the 'windows' of human experience to discover our call to follow God. It is also a testimony to the power of waiting—as people wait for Christmas through the Advent season, and as the birth of Messiah was awaited through the centuries. Waiting can be difficult at times, but Christmas proves the value of patience and of taking time to stop, to look out, to listen.

Margaret Silf is an ecumenical Christian, committed to working across and beyond the denominational divides. Her previous books on Christian spirituality include *Landmarks*, *Taste and See*, *Wayfaring* (all published by DLT) and *Sacred Spaces* (Lion).

The following extract is taken from the book's Introduction.

The First of December, and Christmas is just around the corner! It's the season of expectation, of hope, of anticipation. A season of dreams, and, for Christians, a season where the deepest dream of all humankind meets, face to face, with God's own dream for God's creation, made visible and tangible to everyone who seeks.

One of my most abiding memories is of an evening shared with a friend who had experienced a particularly traumatic childhood. We were talking about our favourite fairy stories, and she told me… of how much the story of 'The Little Matchgirl' had come to mean for her, not just in her dreams but in her Christian journeying too.

As she retold the story, it came to life in a way that reflects, for me, something of the spirit of this Advent journey. The little matchgirl was a young child, undernourished and very poor. She earned her daily bread by selling matches, but the earnings were sparse, and at home a cruel father was waiting to punish her if she failed to bring home enough money. One dark winter night she was standing in her usual place, shivering, and gazing at the lighted windows of the big houses all around her, catching fleeting glimpses of all that was going on inside those rooms—the preparations for Christmas, the lovely gifts, the bright decorations, the happy faces, the smell of Christmas puddings and roasting goose.

All she had was a box of matches… 'Dare I strike one?' she wondered. She took out a match, and struck it, gazing for a few brief moments into its blaze of light. As she did so, she imagined that it was one of those lighted windows. She looked inside, in her imagination, and entered into a warm room where loving friends might welcome her. Another match; another scene. Another window to look into. Perhaps a fine dinner set out for a family. The crackling of the goose, the aroma of mince pies. Food and shelter. And so she continued, until she came to the last match in the box.

The story has a bittersweet ending. As she strikes her last match, the little matchgirl sees a shooting star falling across the night sky, and her granny is standing there, smiling, waiting to gather the child into her arms and carry her home to heaven. The frozen child is discovered the next morning, with an empty matchbox in her hands and a deep, contented smile across her white face.

This Advent journey invites you to share something of the magic and mystery of what it means to look into some of your own 'lighted windows'… During the first three weeks of the journey, we look, day by day, into a series of windows opening up into glimpses of how we might discover God's guidance in our lives, how we might become more trusting of that guidance, and how we might catch something of God's wisdom. During Christmas week, the 'windows' open wide, inviting us to enter the heart of the mystery of God's coming to earth. And as the journey moves on through to the turning of the year, and the feast of the Epiphany, the windows turn into doors, through which we are sent out again into a world that is waiting—and longing—for the touch of God's love upon its broken heart.

Heaven's Morning
Rethinking the destination

DAVID WINTER

pb, 9780857464767, £7.99

The Bible, especially the New Testament, has plenty to say about resurrection and heaven, but what does it actually mean in practice? David Winter's *Heaven's Morning* explores the biblical teaching on what happens after death and considers what difference this can make to our lives, day by day. Winter, one of the UK's most celebrated Christian authors, proves that eternity can be an empowering source of hope to our sceptical, anxious world, and clarifies what is waiting for us—just beyond.

David Winter is one of the UK's most popular and long established Christian writers and broadcasters. He has written many books over the last 60 years, including *At the End of the Day*, *Facing the Darkness, Finding the Light* and *Journey to Jerusalem* for BRF. He also writes for *New Daylight* and contributed regularly to Radio 4's *Thought for the Day* from 1989 to 2012.

St Aidan's Way of Mission
Celtic insights for a post-Christian world

RAY SIMPSON with BRENT LYONS-LEE

pb, 9780857464859, £7.99

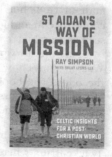

Surveying the life and times of Aidan of Lindisfarne, this book brings great insight not only into the character of this complex Celtic man but also into missional approaches that can inspire outreach and discipleship for today's church. As in his previous BRF book, *Hilda of Whitby*, Ray Simpson shows that such figures from past centuries can provide models for Christian life and witness today. Combining historical fact and spiritual teaching, he introduces St Aidan more fully than ever before.

Revd Ray Simpson is a founder of the international new monastic movement known as The Community of Aidan and Hilda and is principal tutor of its Celtic Christian Studies programmes. He has written more than 30 books on spirituality and lives on Lindisfarne, offering a ministry of counsel and support to visitors, especially those in church leadership. He leads retreats on several continents.

Revd Brent Lyons-Lee contributes material from an Australian cross-cultural mission perspective. He is part of the Baptist Union Mission Catalyst team (Victoria, Australia) and a member of The Community of Aidan and Hilda, and has co-written with Ray a book that explores indigenous mission in Australia: *Celtic Spirituality in an Australian Landscape* (St Aidan Press).

Confidence in the Living God
David and Goliath revisited

ANDREW WATSON

pb, 9780857464828, £7.99

Confidence lies at the heart of society, determining the success or failure of the economy, the government, schools, churches and individuals. As Christians, we are called to proclaim our faith in God, but how can we maintain this confidence in an increasingly secularised culture where faith is often seen as marginal, embarrassing or even downright dangerous?

Using the story of David and Goliath as his starting point, Andrew Watson shows how the Lord can indeed be our confidence, whatever the odds. The book includes a discussion guide and is ideal as a whole-church course on the subject of confidence.

Andrew Watson is Bishop of Guildford and author of *The Fourfold Leadership of Jesus* and *The Way of the Desert*, a BRF Lent book. He was previously Bishop of Aston and vicar of St Stephen's, East Twickenham, where he helped pioneer three church plants.

To order a copy of any of these books, please use the order form opposite. BRF books are also available from your local Christian bookshop or from **www.brfonline.org.uk**.

BRF PUBLICATIONS ORDER FORM

To order our resources online, please visit **www.brfonline.org.uk**

Please send me the following book(s):	Quantity	Price	Total
432 3 **Lighted Windows** Margaret Silf	_____	£7.99	_____
500 9 **Could This Be God?** Brian Harris	_____	£9.99	_____
524 5 **Quiet Spaces Prayer Journal**	_____	£9.99	_____
476 7 **Heaven's Morning** David Winter	_____	£7.99	_____
485 9 **St Aidan's Way of Mission** Ray Simpson	_____	£7.99	_____
482 8 **Confidence in the Living God** Andrew Watson	_____	£7.99	_____
221 3 **Travellers of the Heart** Michael Mitton	_____	£7.99	_____
180 3 **Welcoming the Way of the Cross** Barbara Mosse	_____	£7.99	_____
Quiet Spaces FREE sample copy	_____	£0.00	_____

Total cost of books £ _____

Donation £ _____

Postage and packing (*see overleaf*) £ _____

TOTAL £ _____

Account no. _____

Title _____ First name/initials _____ Surname _____

Address _____

_____ Postcode _____

Telephone _____ Email _____

Total enclosed £ _____ (cheques should be made payable to 'BRF')

Please charge my Mastercard ☐ Visa ☐ Debit card ☐ with £ _____

Card no. ☐☐☐☐ ☐☐☐☐ ☐☐☐☐ ☐☐☐☐

Valid from ☐☐☐☐ MMYY Expires ☐☐☐☐ MMYY

Security code* ☐☐☐ *Last 3 digits on the reverse of the card
ESSENTIAL IN ORDER TO PROCESS YOUR ORDER

Signature _____ Date ___ / ___ / ___
(essential if paying by credit card)

To read our terms and find out about cancelling your order, please visit www.brfonline.org.uk/terms

Please send your completed form with the appropriate payment to:
BRF, 15 The Chambers, Vineyard, Abingdon OX14 3FE

The Bible Reading Fellowship (BRF) is a Registered Charity (233280). VAT No: GB 238 5574 35

POSTAGE AND PACKING CHARGES			
Order value	UK	Europe	Rest of World
Under £7.00	£1.25	£3.00	£5.50
£7.00–£29.99	£2.25	£5.50	£10.00
£30.00 & over	FREE	Prices on request	

Transforming Lives and Communities

BRF is a charity that is passionate about making a difference through the Christian faith. We want to see lives and communities transformed through our creative programmes and resources for individuals, churches and schools. We are doing this by resourcing:

- **Christian growth and understanding of the Bible.** Through our Bible reading notes, books, digital resources, Quiet Days and other events, we're resourcing individuals, groups and leaders in churches for their own spiritual journey and for their ministry.

- **Church outreach in the local community.** BRF is the home of three programmes that churches are embracing to great effect as they seek to engage with their local communities: Messy Church, Who Let The Dads Out? and The Gift of Years.

- **Teaching Christianity in primary schools.** Our Barnabas in Schools team is working with primary-aged children and their teachers, enabling them to explore Christianity creatively within the school curriculum.

- **Children's and family ministry.** Through our Barnabas in Churches and Faith in Homes websites and published resources, we're working with churches and families, enabling children under 11, and the adults working with them, to explore Christianity creatively and bring the Bible alive.

Do you share our vision?

Sales of our books and Bible reading notes cover the cost of producing them. However, our other programmes are funded primarily by donations, grants and legacies. If you share our vision, would you help us to transform even more lives and communities? Your prayers and financial support are vital for the work that we do.

- You could support BRF's ministry with a one-off gift or regular donation (using the response form on page 153).
- You could consider making a bequest to BRF in your will (page 152).
- You could encourage your church to support BRF as part of your church's giving to home mission—perhaps focusing on a specific area of our ministry, or a particular member of our Barnabas team.
- Most important of all, you could support BRF with your prayers.

The difference a gift in your Will can make

Gifts left in Wills don't need to be huge to help us make a real difference, and for every £1 you give, we will invest 88p back into charitable activities.

BRF's vision is to see lives and communities transformed through the Christian faith. For over 90 years we have been able to do amazing things thanks to the generosity of those who have supported us during their lifetime and through gifts in wills.

One of the fastest growing areas of our work is Messy Church. Messy Church reaches people of all ages who have often never set foot in a church before, by being 'church' differently. It is being delivered in a variety of contexts in local communities, including care homes, prisons and schools, in inner city and rural areas. Week by week we are seeing new Messy Churches starting up across the UK and around the globe, and across all major church denominations. We estimate that over 500,000 people are attending Messy Church each month.

A gift in your will could help fund the growth, development and sustainability of programmes like BRF's Messy Church for many years to come. Just imagine what we could do over the next 90 years with your help.

For further information about making a gift to BRF in your will, please contact Sophie Aldred on 01865 319700 or email fundraising@brf.org.uk.

Whatever you can do or give, we thank you for your support.

SHARING OUR VISION – MAKING A GIFT

I would like to make a gift to support BRF. Please use my gift for:

☐ where it is needed most ☐ Barnabas Children's Ministry

☐ Messy Church ☐ Who Let The Dads Out? ☐ The Gift of Years

Title	First name/initials	Surname
Address		
		Postcode
Email		
Telephone		Date

giftaid it **You can add an extra 25p to every £1 you give.**

Please treat as Gift Aid donations all qualifying gifts of money made

☐ today, ☐ in the past four years, ☐ and in the future.

I am a UK taxpayer and understand that if I pay less Income Tax and/or Capital Gains Tax in the current tax year than the amount of Gift Aid claimed on all my donations, it is my responsibility to pay any difference.

☐ **My donation does not qualify for Gift Aid.**

Please notify BRF if you want to cancel this Gift Aid declaration, change your name or address, or you no longer pay sufficient tax on your income and/or capital gains

Please complete other side of form ➡

Please return to:
BRF, 15 The Chambers, Vineyard, Abingdon OX14 3FE

The Bible Reading Fellowship (BRF) is a Registered Charity (233280). VAT No: GB 238 5574 35

SHARING OUR VISION – MAKING A GIFT

Regular Giving

By Direct Debit:

☐ I would like to make a regular gift of £ [   ] per month/quarter/year.
   Please also complete the Direct Debit instruction on page 159.

By Standing Order:
Please contact Priscilla Kew, tel. 01235 462305; priscilla.kew@brf.org.uk

One-off Donation

Please accept my gift of:

☐ £10   ☐ £50   ☐ £100   Other £ [   ]

by (*delete as appropriate*):

☐ Cheque/Charity Voucher payable to 'BRF'

☐ Mastercard/Visa/Debit card/Charity Card

Name on card

Card no. [ ][ ][ ][ ] [ ][ ][ ][ ] [ ][ ][ ][ ] [ ][ ][ ][ ]

Valid from [M][M][Y][Y]   Expires [M][M][Y][Y]

Security code* [ ][ ][ ]   *Last 3 digits on the reverse of the card
ESSENTIAL IN ORDER TO PROCESS THE PAYMENT

Signature | Date

We like to acknowledge all donations. However, if you do not wish to receive an acknowledgement, please tick here ☐

← Please complete other side of form

Please return to:
BRF, 15 The Chambers, Vineyard, Abingdon OX14 3FE

The Bible Reading Fellowship (BRF) is a Registered Charity (233280). VAT No: GB 238 5574 35

ND0316

How to encourage Bible reading in your church

BRF has been helping individuals connect with the Bible for over 90 years. We want to support churches as they seek to encourage church members into regular Bible reading.

Order a Bible reading resources pack

This pack is designed to give your church the tools to publicise our Bible reading notes. It includes:

• Sample Bible reading notes for your congregation to try.
• Publicity resources, including a poster.
• A church magazine feature about Bible reading notes.

The pack is free, but we welcome a £5 donation to cover the cost of postage. If you require a pack to be sent outside the UK or require a specific number of sample Bible reading notes, please contact us for postage costs. More information about what the current pack contains is available on our website.

How to order and find out more

• Visit www.biblereadingnotes.org.uk/for-churches
• Telephone BRF on 01865 319700 between 9.15 am and 5.30 pm
• Write to us at BRF, 15 The Chambers, Vineyard, Abingdon OX14 3FE

Keep informed about our latest initiatives

We are continuing to develop resources to help churches encourage people into regular Bible reading, wherever they are on their journey. Join our email list at www.biblereadingnotes.org.uk/helpingchurches to stay informed about the latest initiatives that your church could benefit from.

Introduce a friend to our notes

We can send information about our notes and current prices for you to pass on. Please contact us.

NEW DAYLIGHT INDIVIDUAL SUBSCRIPTION FORM

> All our Bible reading notes can be ordered online by visiting
> **www.biblereadingnotes.org.uk/subscriptions**

[ ] I would like to take out a subscription:

Title _____ First name/initials _____ Surname _____

Address _____

_____ Postcode _____

Telephone _____ Email _____

Please send New Daylight beginning with the January 2017 / May 2017 / September 2017 issue (*delete as appropriate*):

(*please tick box*)	UK	Europe	Rest of World
New Daylight	[ ] £16.35	[ ] £24.90	[ ] £28.20
New Daylight 3-year subscription	[ ] £43.20	N/A	N/A
New Daylight DELUXE	[ ] £20.70	[ ] £33.75	[ ] £40.50

Total enclosed £ _____ (cheques should be made payable to 'BRF')

Please charge my Mastercard [ ] Visa [ ] Debit card [ ] with £ _____

Card no. [ ][ ][ ][ ] [ ][ ][ ][ ] [ ][ ][ ][ ] [ ][ ][ ][ ]

Valid from [M][M] [Y][Y]   Expires [M][M] [Y][Y]

Security code* [ ][ ]   *Last 3 digits on the reverse of the card
ESSENTIAL IN ORDER TO PROCESS YOUR ORDER

Signature _____ Date ____ / ____ / ____

(*essential if paying by credit card*)

To read our terms and find out about cancelling your order, please visit www.brfonline.org.uk/terms

To set up a Direct Debit, please also complete the Direct Debit instruction on page 159 and return it to BRF with this form.

Please send your completed form with the appropriate payment to:
BRF, 15 The Chambers, Vineyard, Abingdon OX14 3FE

The Bible Reading Fellowship (BRF) is a Registered Charity (233280). VAT No: GB 238 5574 35

ND0316

NEW DAYLIGHT GIFT SUBSCRIPTION FORM

☐ **I would like to give a gift subscription** (please provide both names and addresses):

Title _____ First name/initials _____ Surname _____

Address _____

_____ Postcode _____

Telephone _____ Email _____

Gift subscription name _____

Gift subscription address _____

_____ Postcode _____

Gift message (20 words max. or include your own gift card):

_____

_____

Please send New Daylight beginning with the January 2017 / May 2017 / September 2017 issue (*delete as appropriate*):

(please tick box)	UK	Europe	Rest of World
New Daylight	☐ £16.35	☐ £24.90	☐ £28.20
New Daylight 3-year subscription	☐ £43.20	N/A	N/A
New Daylight DELUXE	☐ £20.70	☐ £33.75	☐ £40.50

Total enclosed £ _____ (cheques should be made payable to 'BRF')

Please charge my Mastercard ☐ Visa ☐ Debit card ☐ with £ _____

Card no. ☐☐☐☐ ☐☐☐☐ ☐☐☐☐ ☐☐☐☐

Valid from M M Y Y   Expires M M Y Y

Security code* ☐☐☐   *Last 3 digits on the reverse of the card
ESSENTIAL IN ORDER TO PROCESS YOUR ORDER

Signature _____ Date ____ / ____ / ____

(essential if paying by credit card)

To read our terms and find out about cancelling your order, please visit www.brfonline.org.uk/terms

To set up a Direct Debit, please also complete the Direct Debit instruction on page 159 and return it to BRF with this form.

Please send your completed form with the appropriate payment to:
BRF, 15 The Chambers, Vineyard, Abingdon OX14 3FE

The Bible Reading Fellowship (BRF) is a Registered Charity (233280). VAT No: GB 238 5574 35

DIRECT DEBIT PAYMENT

You can pay for your annual subscription to our Bible reading notes using Direct Debit. You need only give your bank details once, and the payment is made automatically every year until you cancel it. If you would like to pay by Direct Debit, please use the form opposite, entering your BRF account number under 'Reference'.

You are fully covered by the Direct Debit Guarantee:

The Direct Debit Guarantee

- This Guarantee is offered by all banks and building societies that accept instructions to pay Direct Debits.

- If there are any changes to the amount, date or frequency of your Direct Debit, The Bible Reading Fellowship will notify you 10 working days in advance of your account being debited or as otherwise agreed. If you request The Bible Reading Fellowship to collect a payment, confirmation of the amount and date will be given to you at the time of the request.

- If an error is made in the payment of your Direct Debit, by The Bible Reading Fellowship or your bank or building society, you are entitled to a full and immediate refund of the amount paid from your bank or building society.

- If you receive a refund you are not entitled to, you must pay it back when The Bible Reading Fellowship asks you to.

- You can cancel a Direct Debit at any time by simply contacting your bank or building society. Written confirmation may be required. Please also notify us.

The Bible Reading Fellowship

Instruction to your bank or building society to pay by Direct Debit

Please fill in the whole form using a ballpoint pen and return it to:
BRF, 15 The Chambers, Vineyard, Abingdon OX14 3FE

Service User Number: | 5 | 5 | 8 | 2 | 2 | 9 |

Name and full postal address of your bank or building society

To: The Manager	Bank/Building Society
Address	
	Postcode

Name(s) of account holder(s)

Branch sort code

Bank/Building Society account number

Reference

Instruction to your Bank/Building Society
Please pay The Bible Reading Fellowship Direct Debits from the account detailed in this instruction, subject to the safeguards assured by the Direct Debit Guarantee. I understand that this instruction may remain with The Bible Reading Fellowship and, if so, details will be passed electronically to my bank/building society.

Signature(s)

Banks and Building Societies may not accept Direct Debit instructions for some types of account.

This page is for your notes.